Center for Creative Photography, University of Arizona, Tucson

Fotomuseum, Münchner Stadtmuseum, Munich
Stadtgalerie, Saarbrücken
Musée de l'Elysée, Lausanne
AR/GE Kunst, Bozen/Bolzano
Southeast Center for Contemporary Art, Winston-Salem

ANN MANDELBAUM
NEW WORK

Texts by Trudy Wilner Stack and Rudolf Schmitz

EDITION STEMMLE

Contents

Anatomy Lesson
Trudy Wilner Stack

"This part of France is delicately colorless, and faintly metallic in texture; if I adjust my position slightly, I may find my own fragmentary image reflected in the darker parts of the scene before me."

Hollis Frampton

Stick out your tongue, close one eye, and reach toward the other with your mouth's slimy protuberance. Look down. This is a curiosity that permits us to speak, to taste, to ingest, to salivate, and to kiss deeply. Marvelous tool, essential sensory organ. But really look at it. How strange this wet and fleshy muscle is with its pimpled surface, its primal animation, its unsettling hybrid identity of extremity and internal organ. The art of Ann Mandelbaum endows tongues and their gatekeeping lips with an autonomous power assumed in the isolation of the photographic frame, in an estrangement from the body both eery and delightful. Her work achieves a transformation of the purpose and effect of anatomical elements in a potent new scrutiny and delineation of our organic selves.

The strangeness and beauty of our body parts is the ground for most of Mandelbaum's work. Her vision is spun from a daringly close look at the most expressive hairs, creased flesh, fingers, ears, nipples, and eyes. She reveres the sensuality and vulnerability of corporeal life, steeped in biological origins and social anxieties. But like children who delight in the magic trick of a wink, a smile, a jiggling belly, or finger play—an extended tongue or open mouth full of food—this artist also exploits the hilarity of our anatomy: the orifices, extremities, the moles, hairs, wrinkles and other features of the skin that help make us. Her view is macroscopic, that is, her subjects are large enough to be seen by the unaided eye, but the focus is so particular through the filter of the camera's macro lens and her refined enlargements, that each visible detail becomes itself a universe of information, feeling, and formal experience—a macrocosm of human mortal material.

"My work seems to follow my own life cycles; the vulnerable years with too many endings; the sensual years with intimacy that comes and goes; the intermittent obsession with aging flesh; and the increased insight of the aging mind."

Despite their beguiling ambiguity and tendency towards abstraction, the photographs of Ann Mandelbaum are derived from the everyday. She looks to her family and friends, a circle of intimates, as models, or more accurately mediums, for her investigations. She finds vegetable matter in the refrigerator, holes in the wall, people blowing bubble gum or drinking milk, at hand. Her material is occasional and private, in the manner of women's writing and art when women were denied public audiences and legitimized contexts. But like the male masters who define art's pantheon, Mandelbaum has developed an aesthetic that is distinctive and recognized in contemporary practice, which has a conceptual, visual and technical style that lends her work critical credence and marketability, at home and in Europe. Her evolution as a successful artist is in sync with her lived experience; hers is a perspective not of superficial sophistication, but earned acumen. If her subjects are quotidian, their aspect as portrayed by Mandelbaum exceeds any ready identification. Bulbous masses and glowing surfaces appear as dense fields, forming landscapes of matte gray tints that rechart the body as both alien terrain and mysteriously familiar ground. Though visual, her images hold a rich blend of the other senses: smell, taste, touch, even sound. They scream and drip and stink and breathe and exude a deceptive tactility.

"The senses are very important to the way I live. I crave exotic tastes and massage and balmy air. In fact, I am obsessed by all textures, sound, and the smell of things. So this is indigenous to my work."

But modifying the messages we receive from our senses are the social constructs that define a less fluid assessment of ourselves. Are we too hairy, too wrinkly, too loose under the chin? What is it about each of us is considered out of place, aberrant, excessive, or uncomfortably feral? What are the accepted standards of beauty and appearance that we may fail to meet? Ann Mandelbaum is admittedly obsessed with troubling features brought on by birthright, age, and ethnicity. Raised by beauticians, her sensitivity to these issues was heightened in an atmosphere of physical appraisal and badgering suggestions on methods for correcting or hiding supposed deficiencies. She was trained to inspect and judge herself and others, and her discriminating attention to physical details now feeds her art. Exploring the drama that lies between fascination and repulsion, Mandelbaum picks and pokes, translating her attentions into seductive prints that throw open questions of self-image and self-examination. Her diffused, luminous, in-your-face portrayals of bodily features and flaws are candid variations on our organism, set somewhere between the make-up mirror, a lover's audit, and a magnified scientific scan. Her conversion of the cosmetic to the cosmic includes a sexual spin, an energy that effectively endows her work with a transmutability both exciting and surprising to viewers. But it is not necessarily the erotic that concerns this artist, though it often preoccupies critics. The slippage between genders that imbues her images—a summoning of androgynous cues—and a refusal to overly identify the body with the blinding idea of intercourse, is brought home when an inventory of her work produces no actual representations of genitalia, buttocks, or women's nipples. By refusing these commonplace subjects (whose apparent potency helped photography unwittingly dismantle public funding of the arts in the United States), Mandelbaum rejects any clear description of the sexual for a less specific evocation that makes her audience more accountable for their own fantasies.

"I am trying to create something that will demand that viewers acknowledge their physical presence, acknowledge their needs, their desires. Many of the pictures can feel too close —there's a resemblance that's unnerving, that's uncanny. Often the forms are so startling that they provoke a response that is not a mind experience until it has been a body experience. It is almost like finding yourself turned on by something you didn't even know you were looking at."

If a passage of flesh can lure our libidos, it can also cause us to squirm in less arousing ways. Mandelbaum's landscapes of the body suggest a panoply of responses to the human package, often with an emphasis on openings, most recently eyes. Rendering the very tool she uses to create her vision, the artist shows us eyes shut, squinting lids, rumpled thin skin trimmed with evenly spaced hairs that gesture in short, slender strokes. They can look like a poorly sutured wound or an embodiment of the idealized innocence of sleep. In one image two eyes abut intimately, their lashes just touching, the lines of their brows and noses luminously outlined in a poignant, intimate seal of skin and hair, a butterfly kiss. In another, a shaving of mica or shard of glass presents a clouded scrim on the eyelid and a thick stand of lashes that point downward, dark like the bushier arch of eyebrow that counterpoints their shape above. A third eye image is a profile, softened in a sensuously smooth but melancholy gray like so many of Mandelbaum's works. It promises the vulnerability and attraction of one open eye's address of another, but again does not deliver, as the angle is too oblique to expose the eyeball itself. Instead we experience a topography of the face, a fuzzy contoured horizon punctuated by two berms of flesh edged in stiff curving hairs—two rows of them—that lean into each other, in and out of focus, effecting a radically new rendition.

"Scanning the body, I am intrigued by the array and size of openings, by the difference between those which beckon and those which repel. I feel thrilled when the eye, for example, provokes these two impulses at the same time, existing as both an opening and a closure. I am looking at that confusing place where, as humans, we don't know whether to enter or retreat, reject or receive."

The photography of Ann Mandelbaum has and continues to extend beyond the scope of the human body. Whether the source of an image is anatomical or not, it is so indistinct or protean that the associations broaden regardless of the trace of realism inscribed on the negative. Her wish is to keep her audience guessing, to push us as she pushes her images, towards boundaries of already suspect origin, towards such a state of receptivity to normal encounters that we make of ourselves and what we experience our own sensory trip, an unpremeditated journey taken with eyes open.

Plates

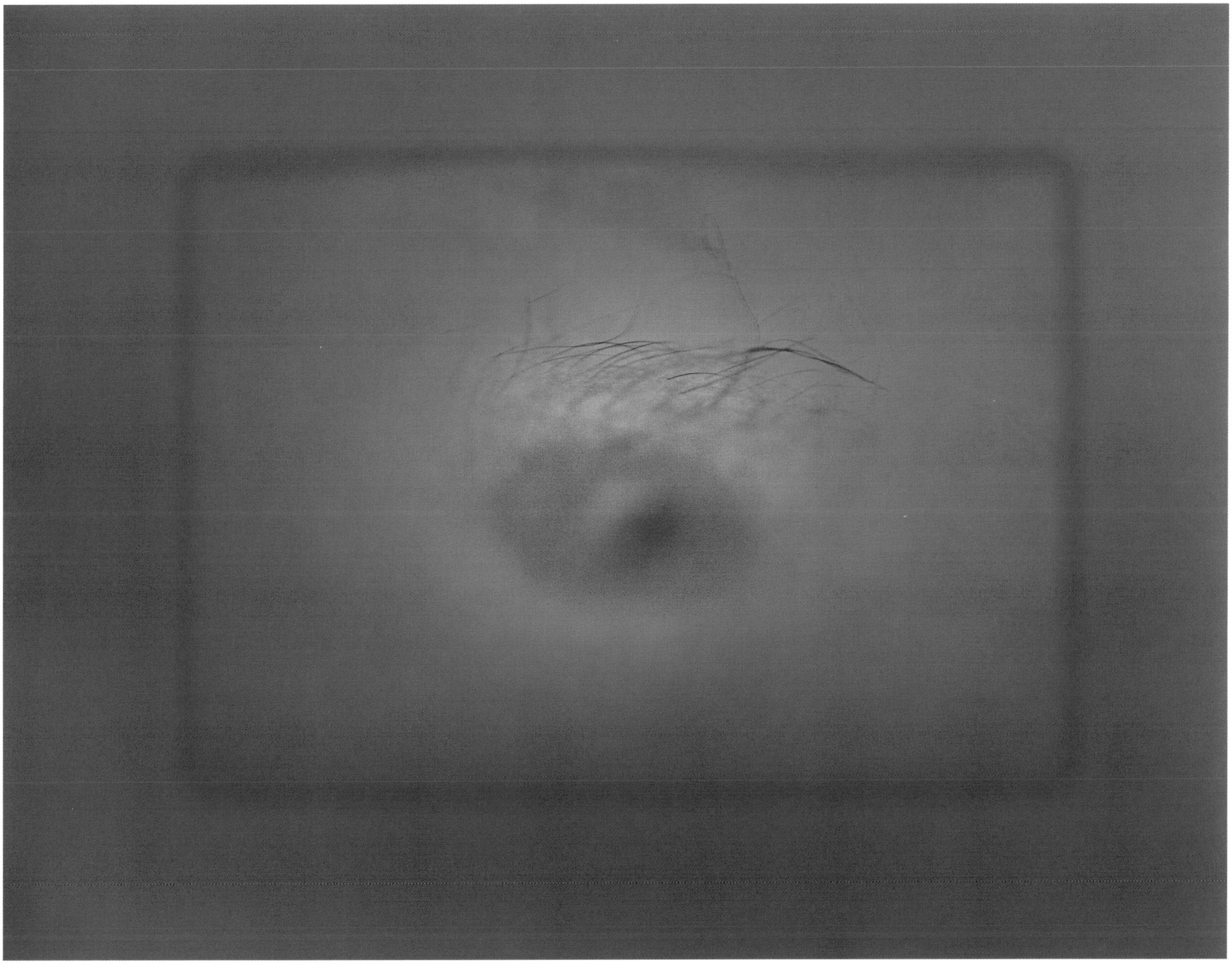

1

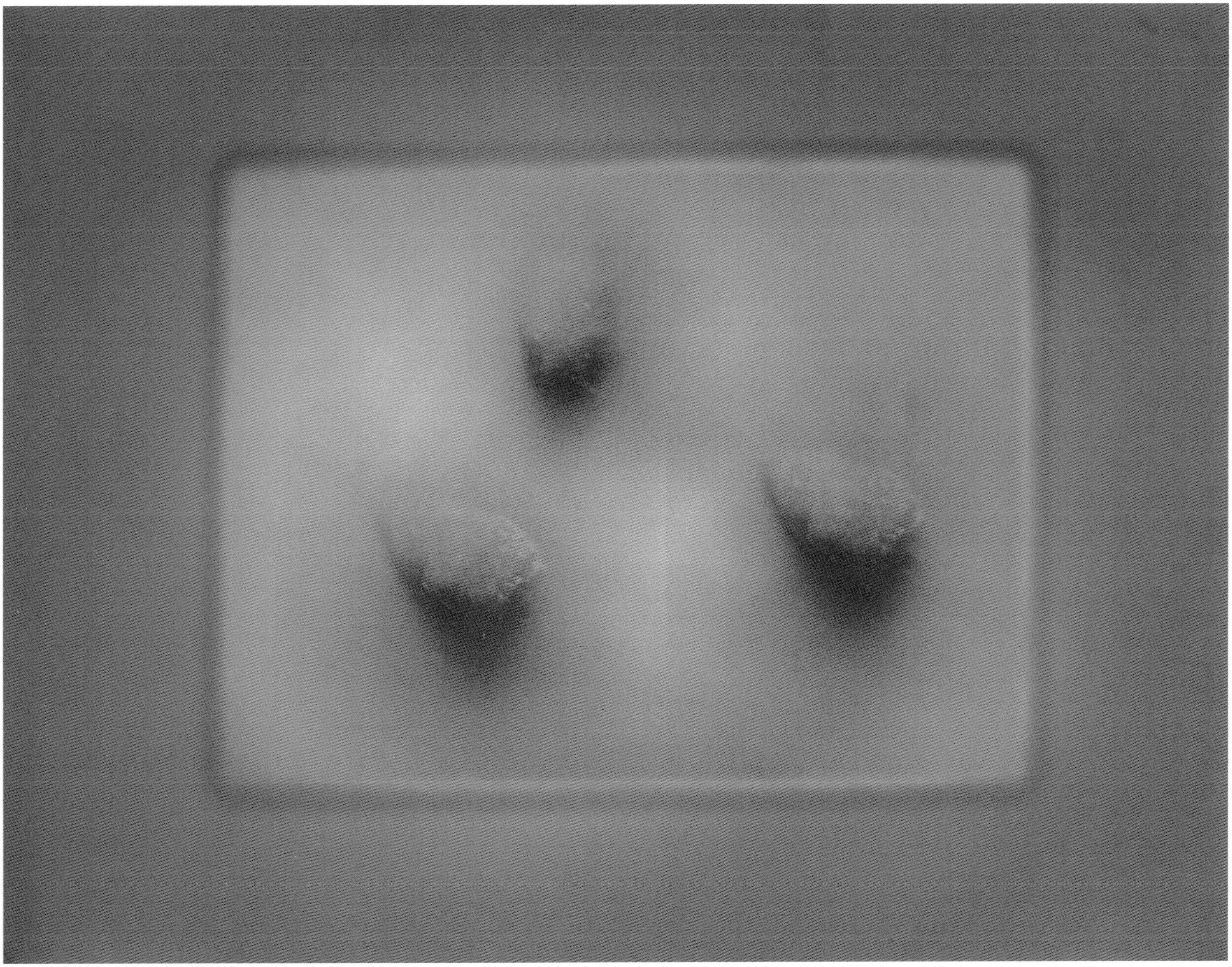

2

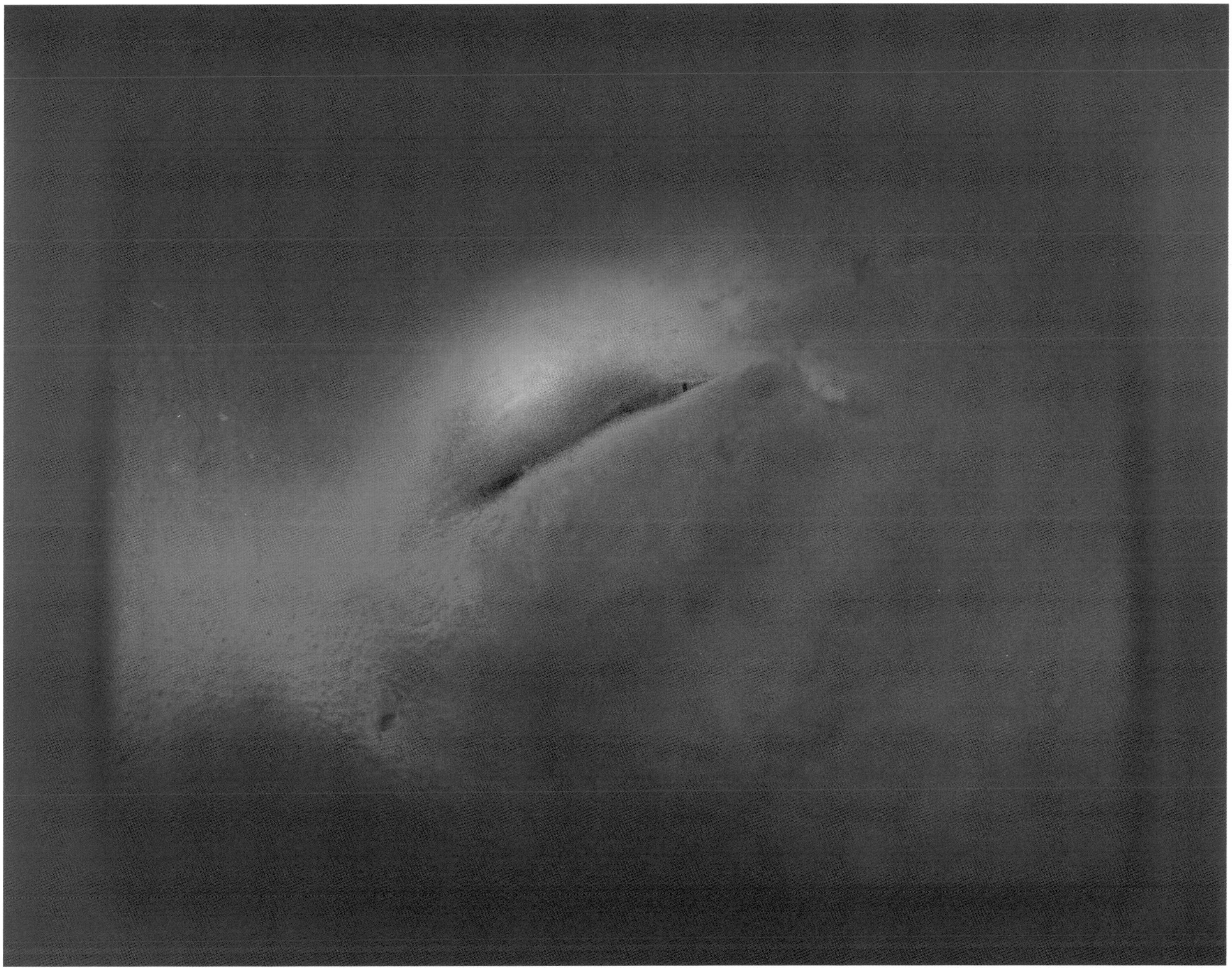

3

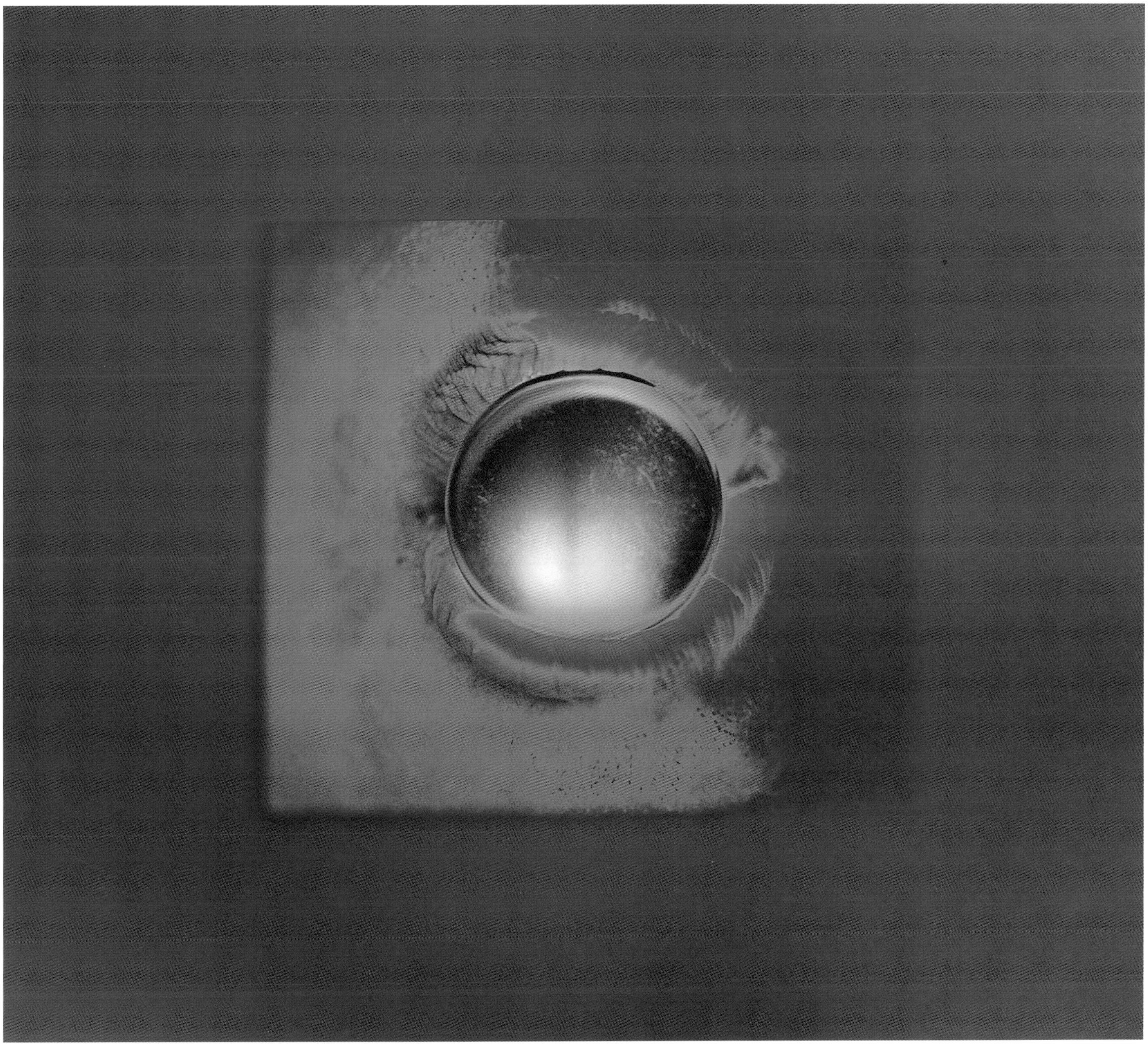

4

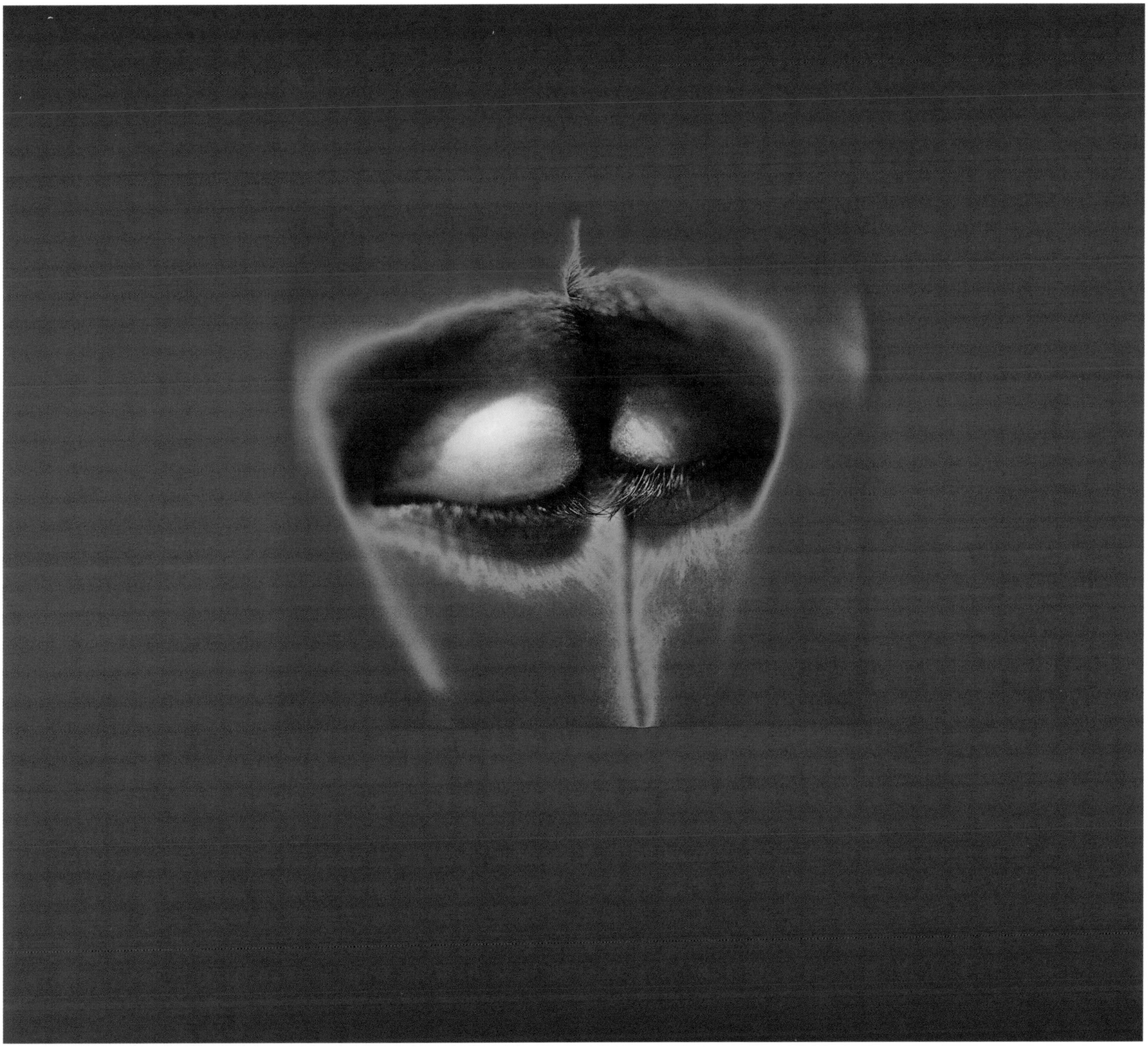

5

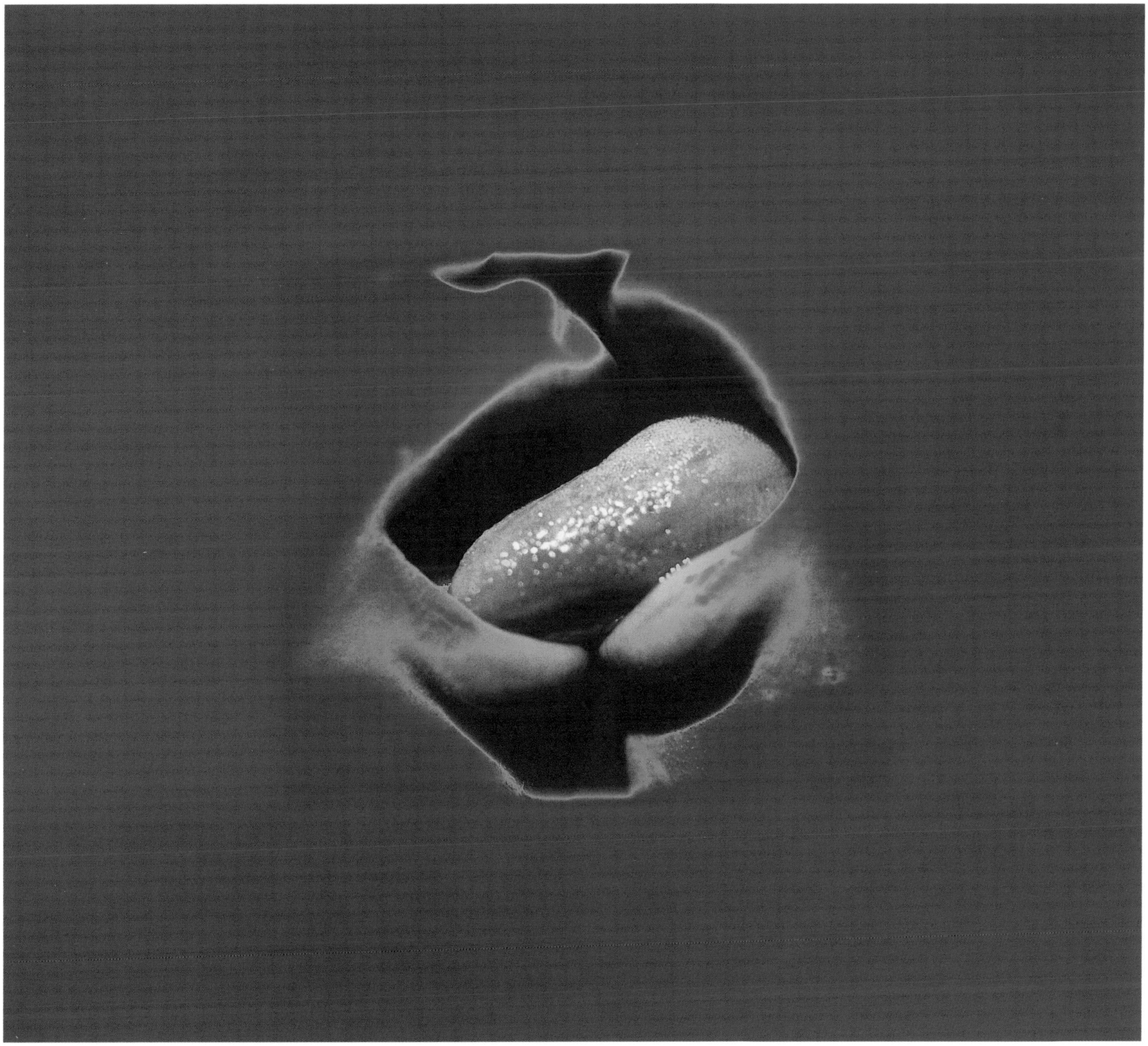

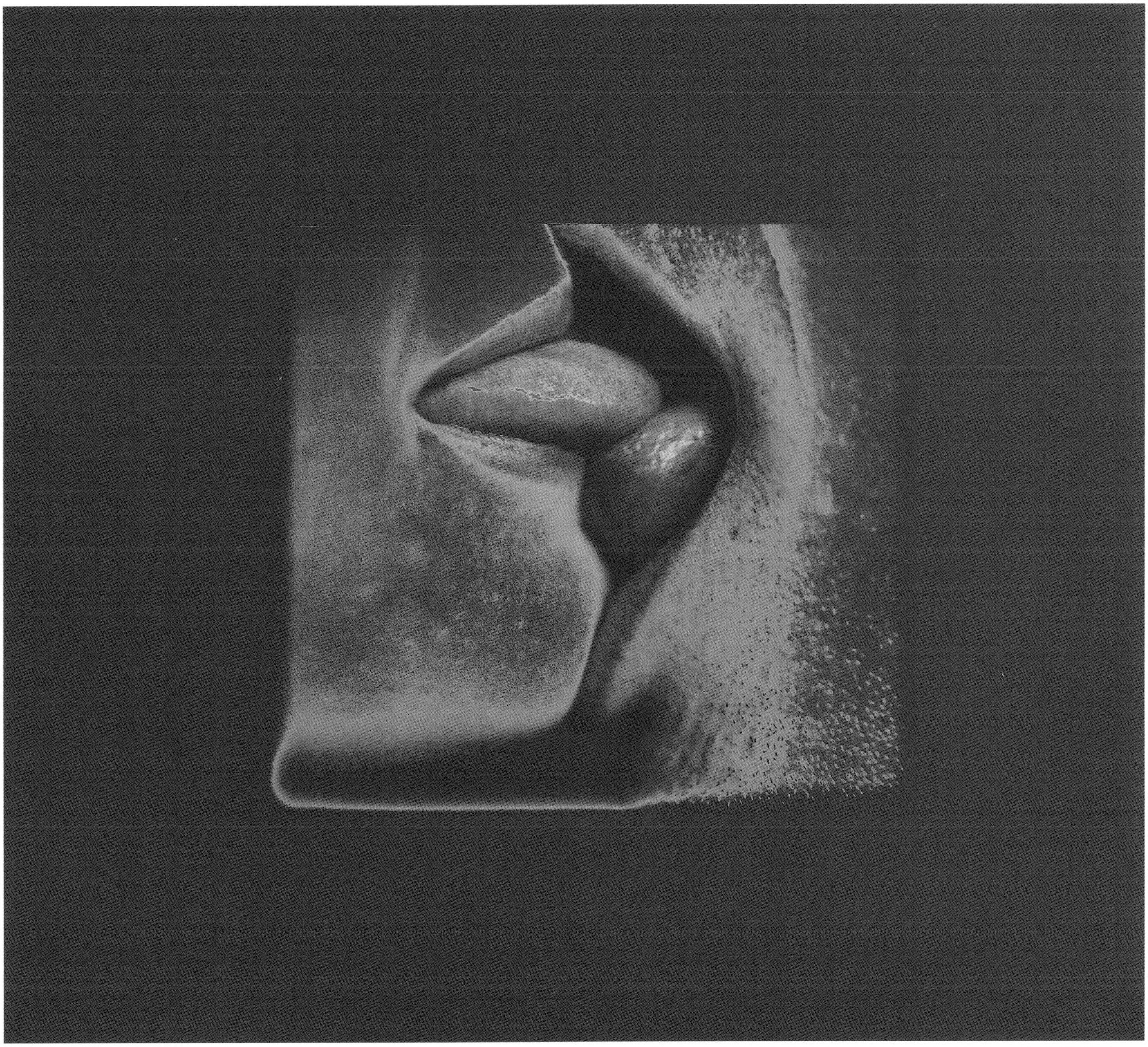

7

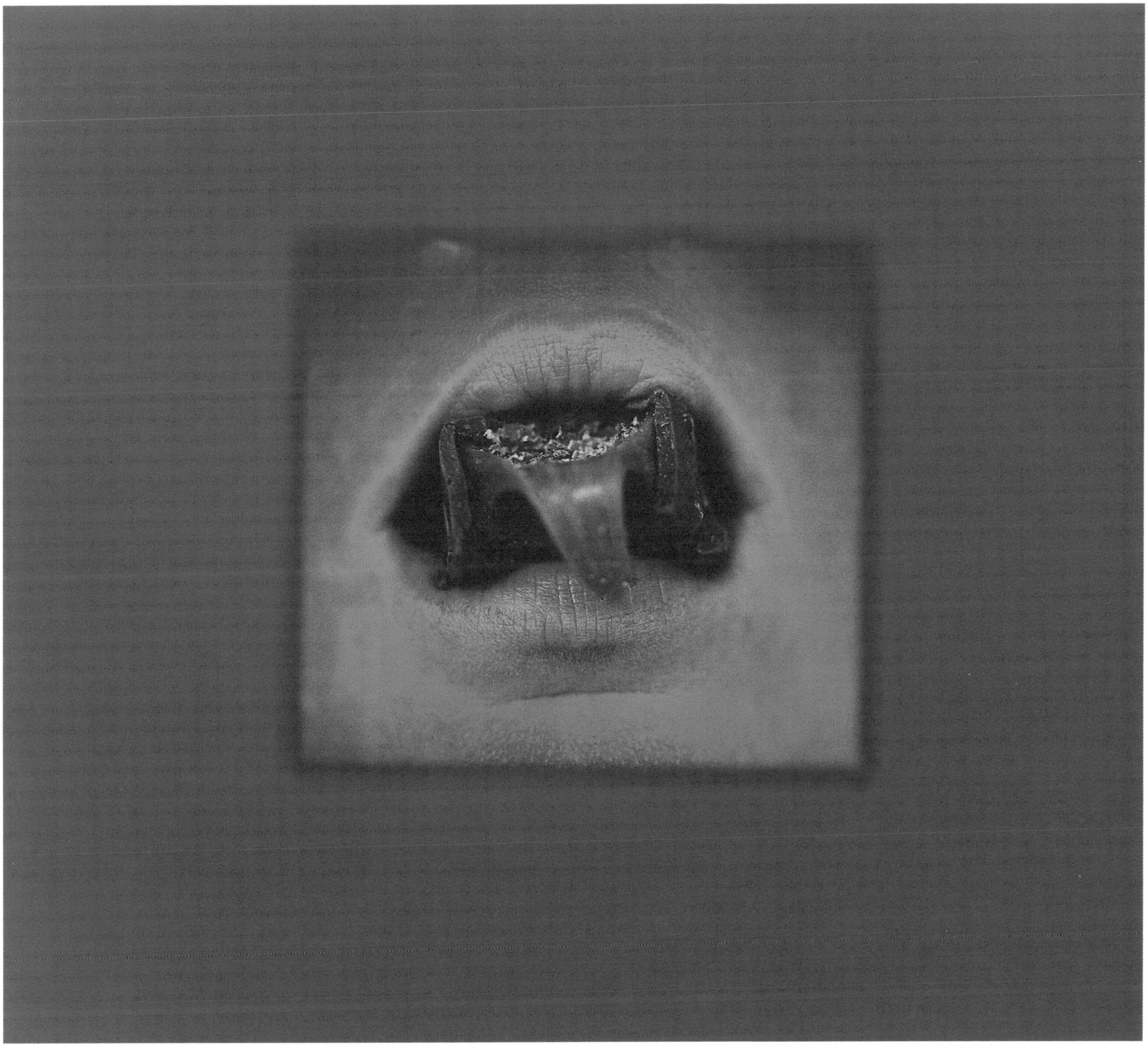

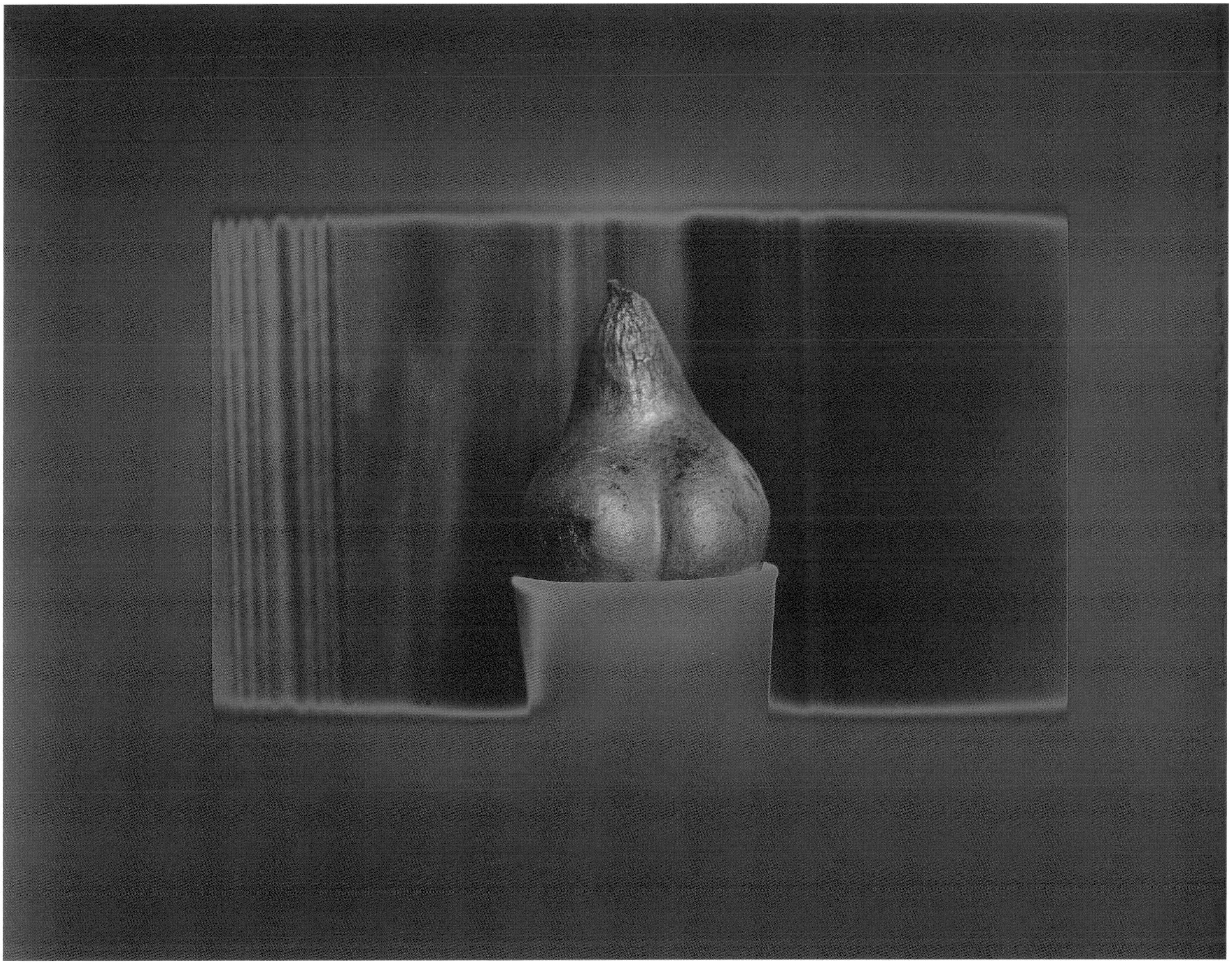

9

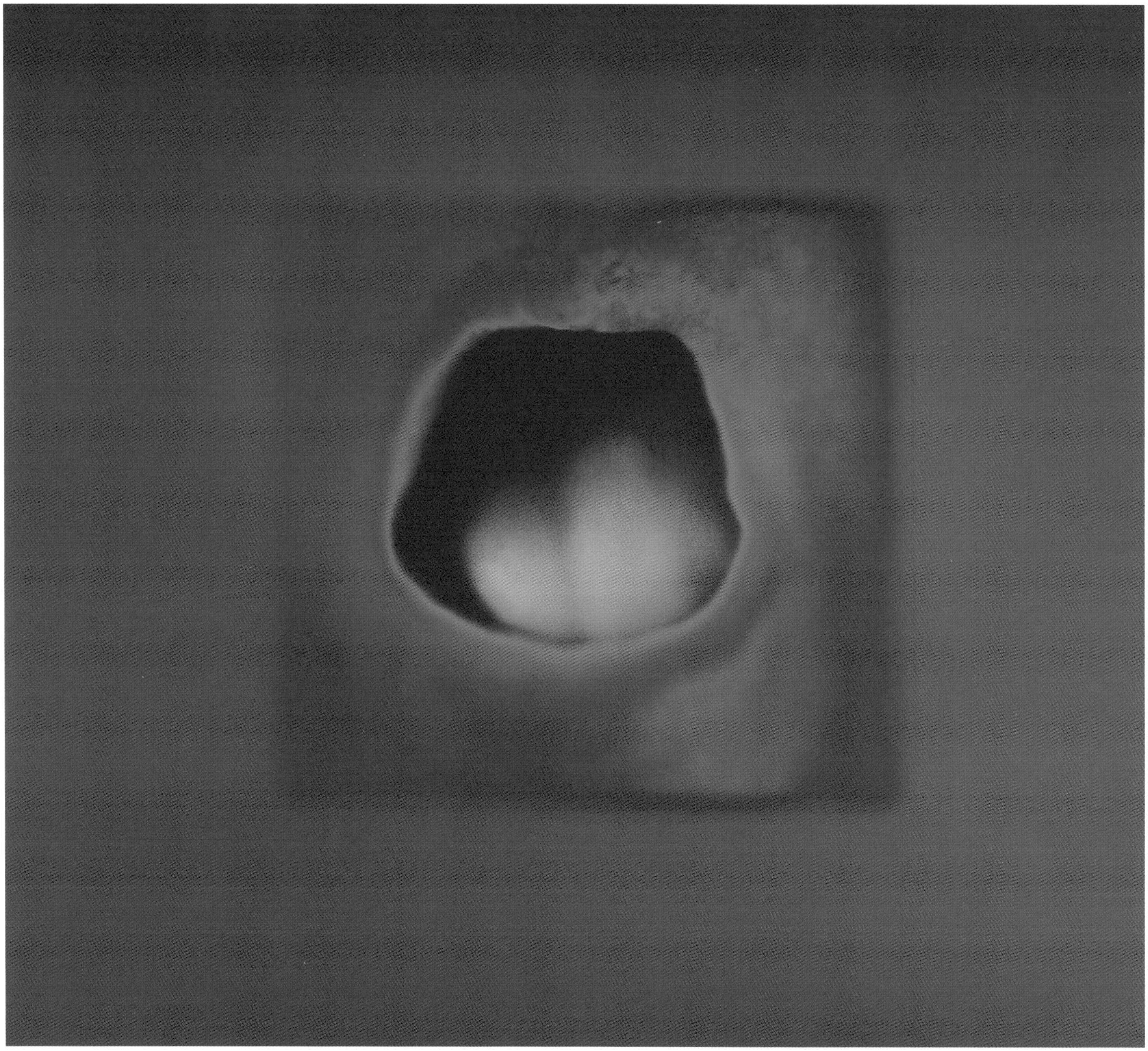

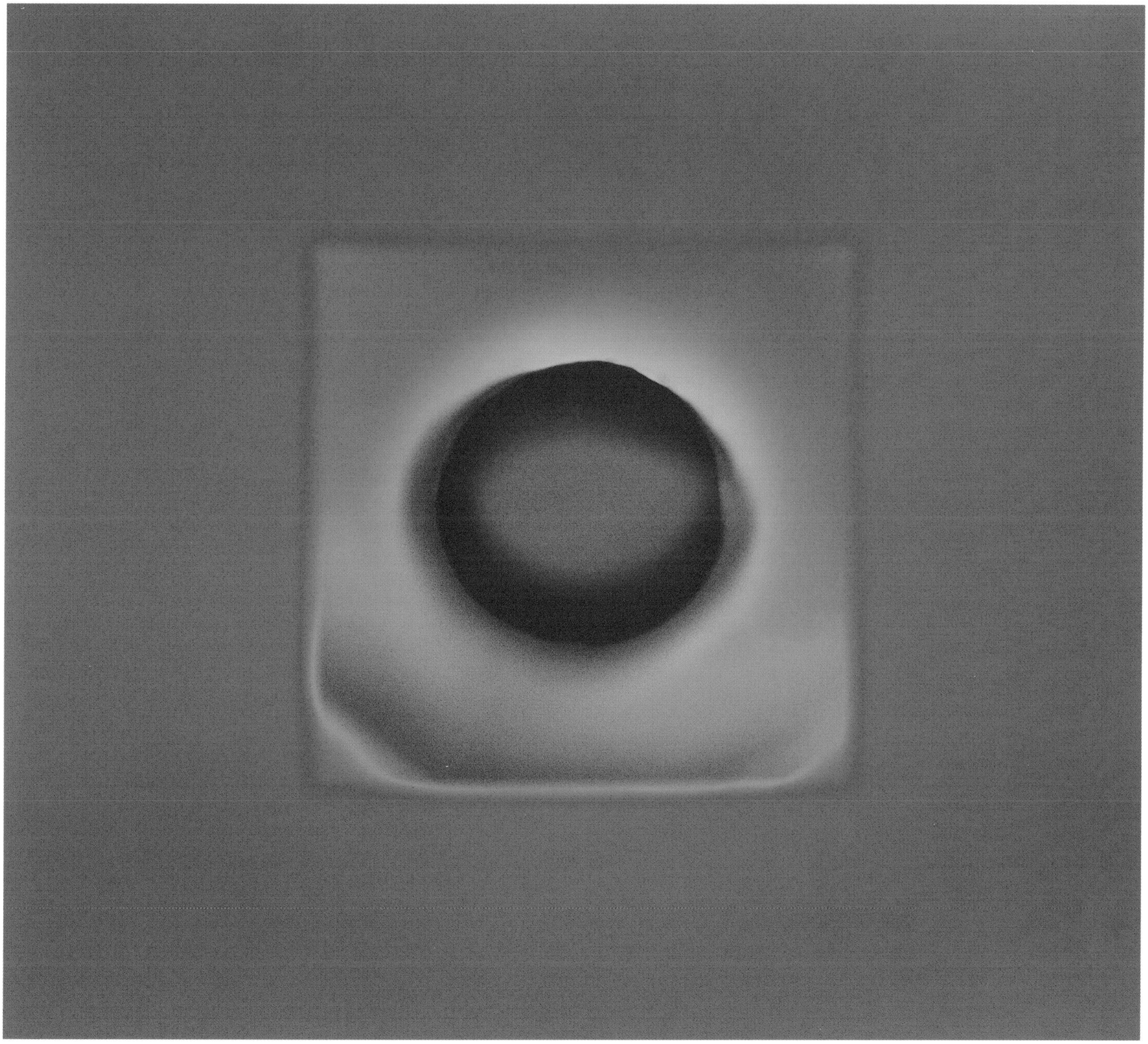

11

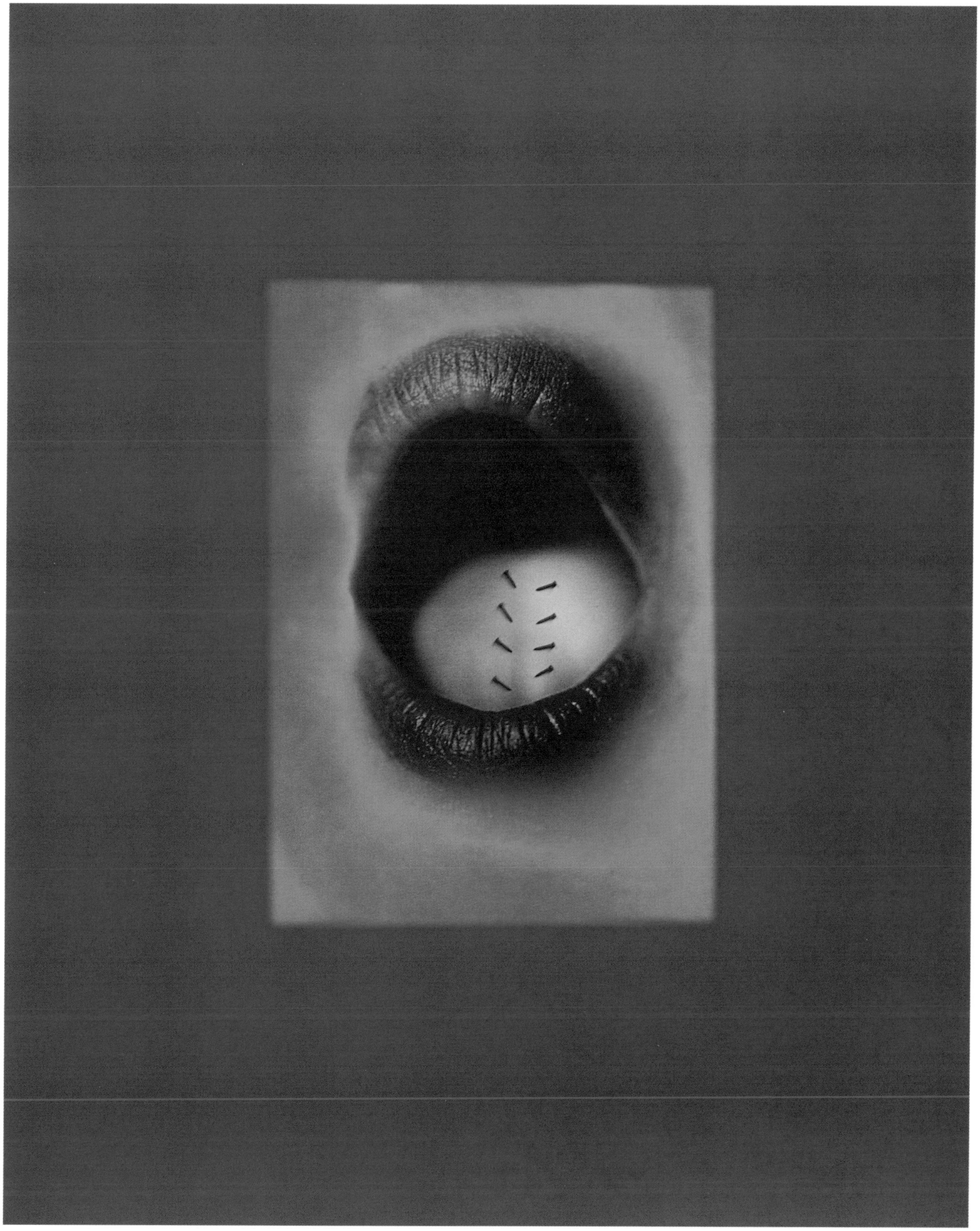

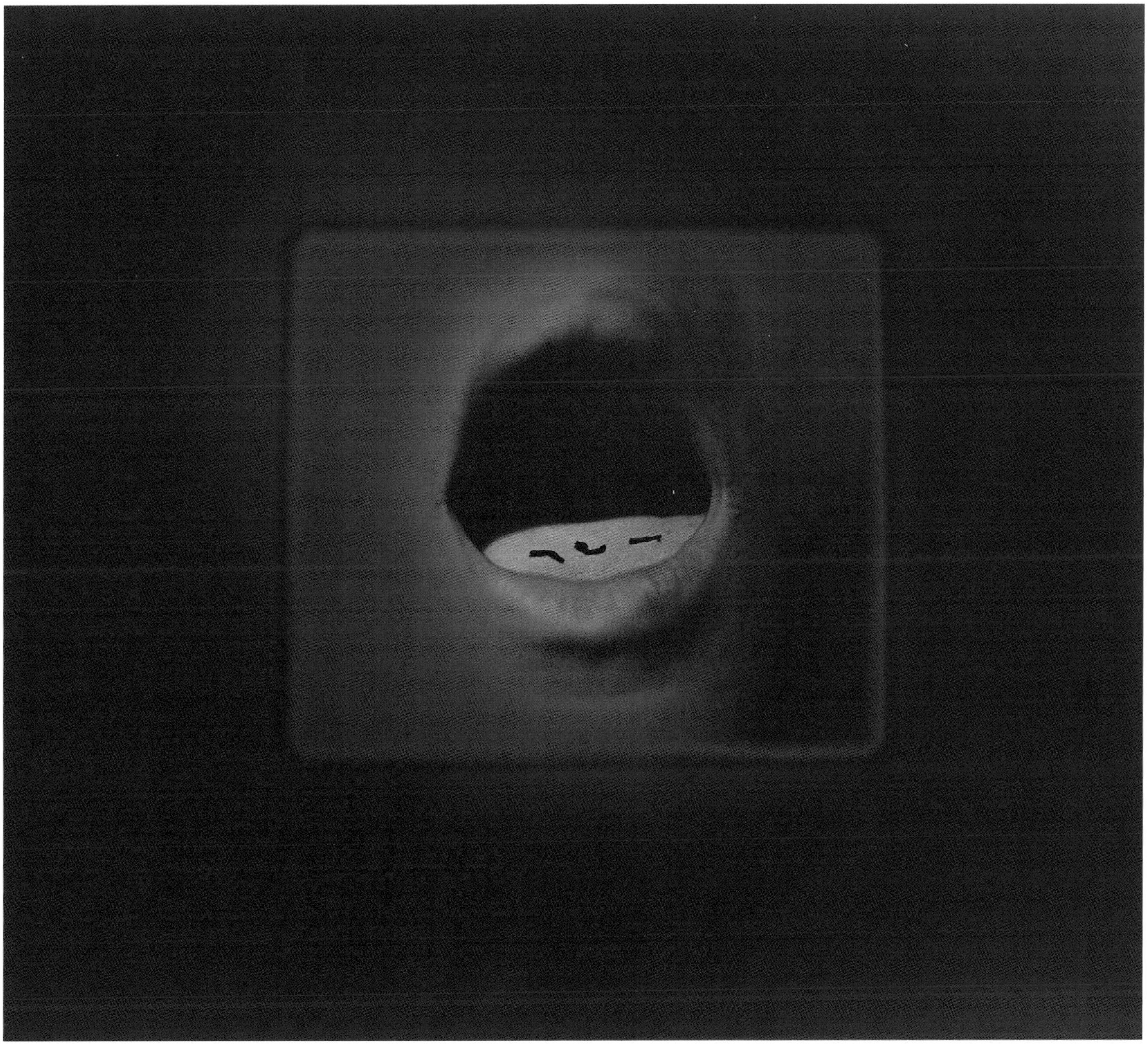

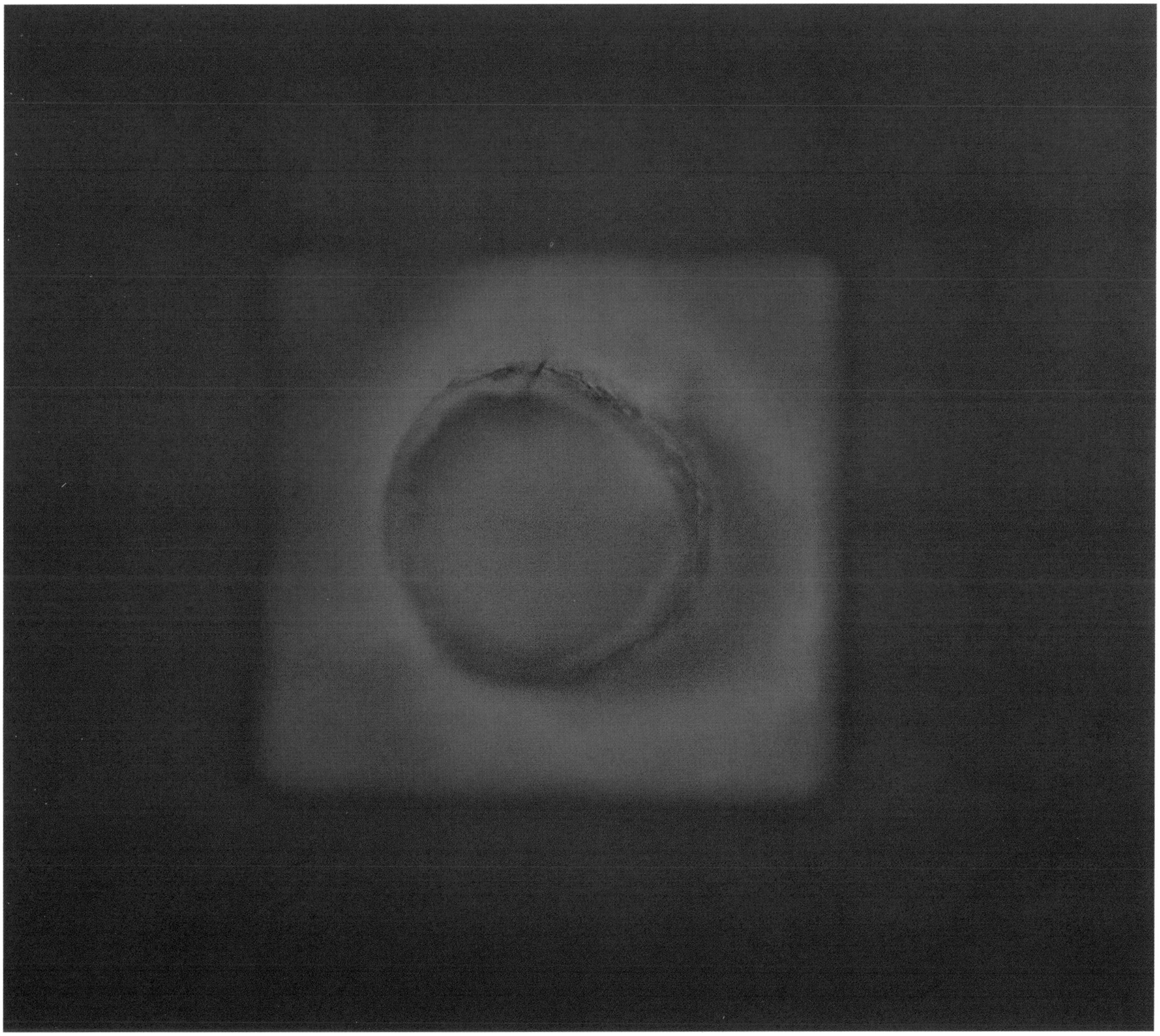

15

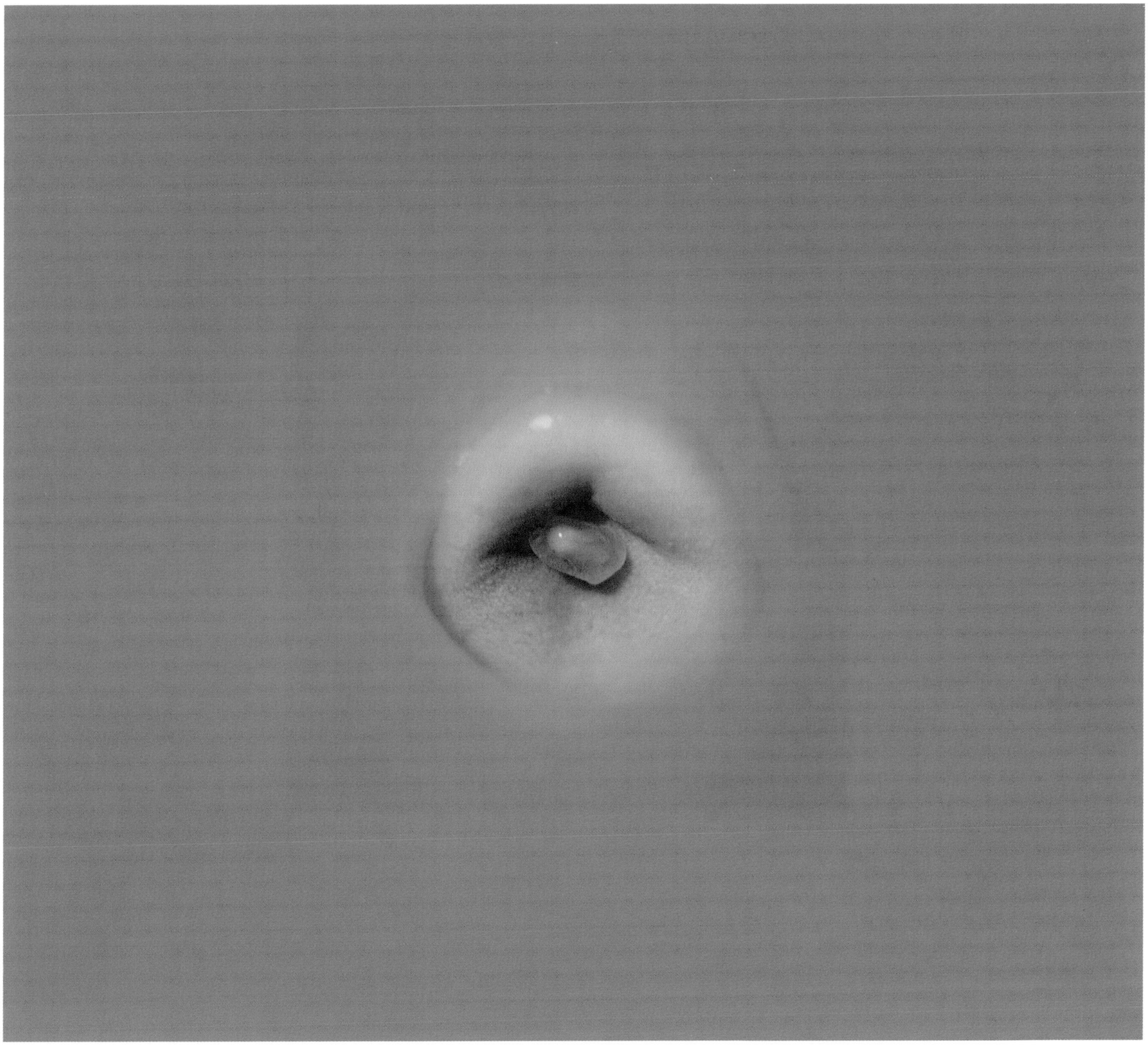

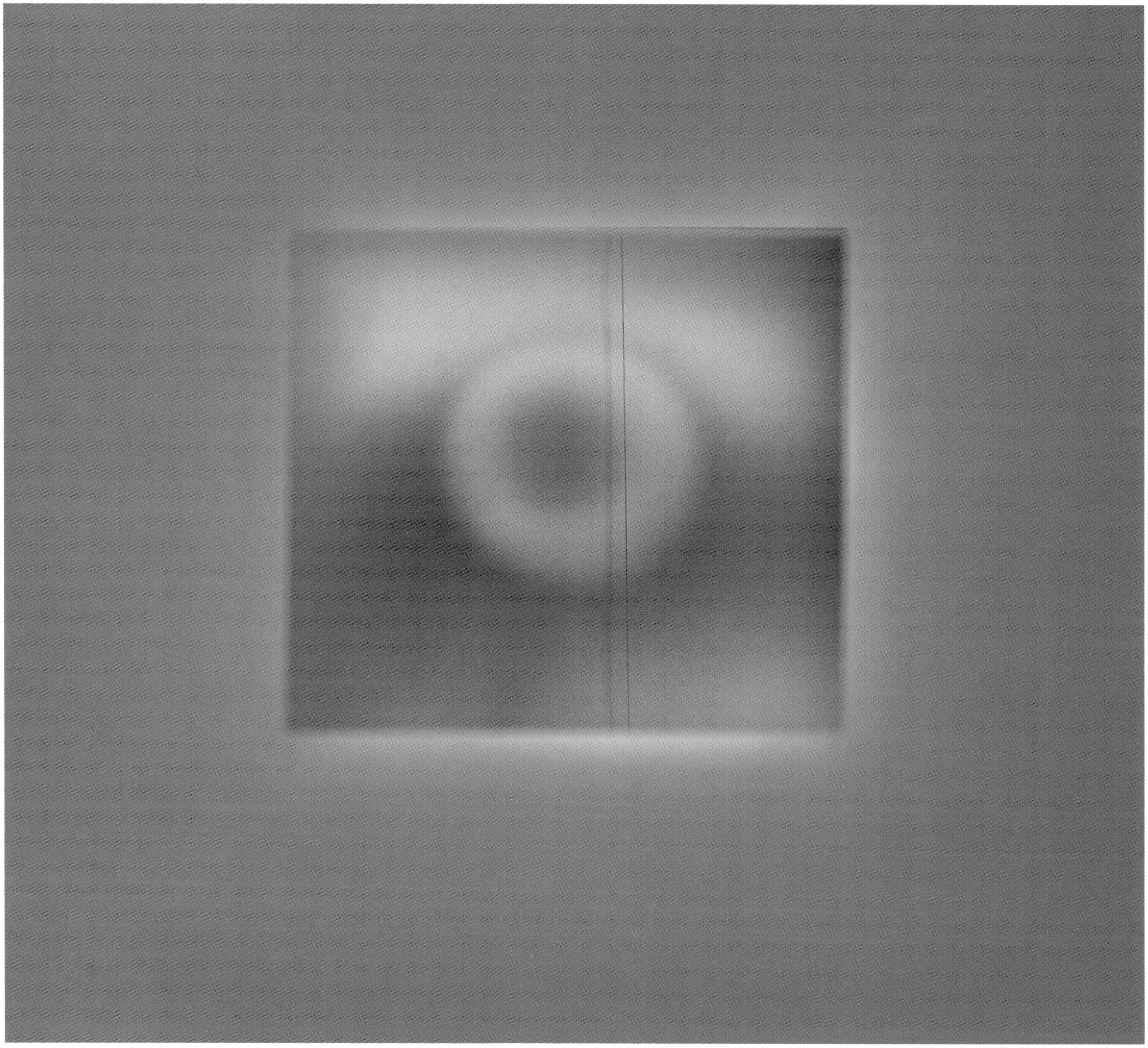

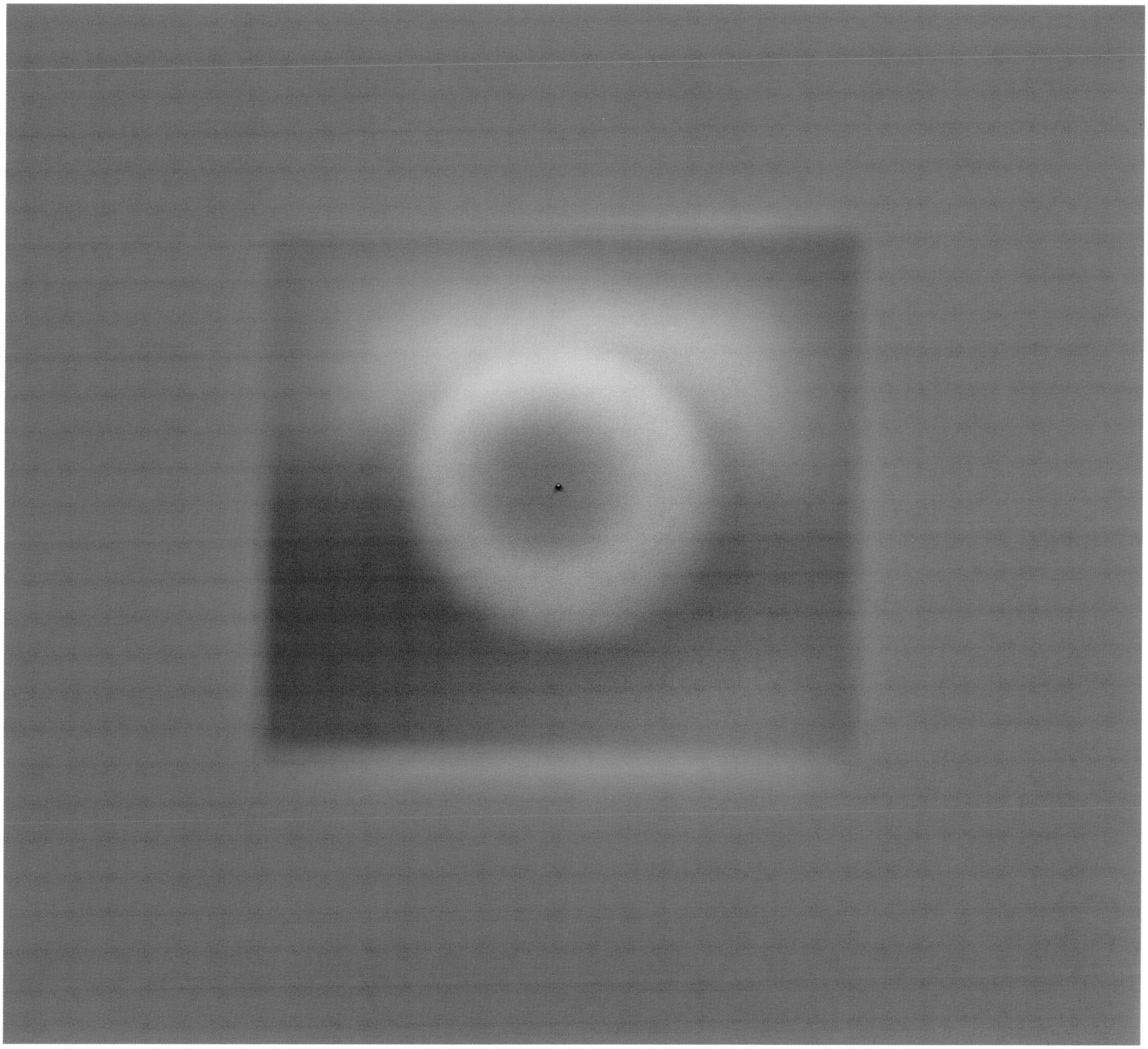

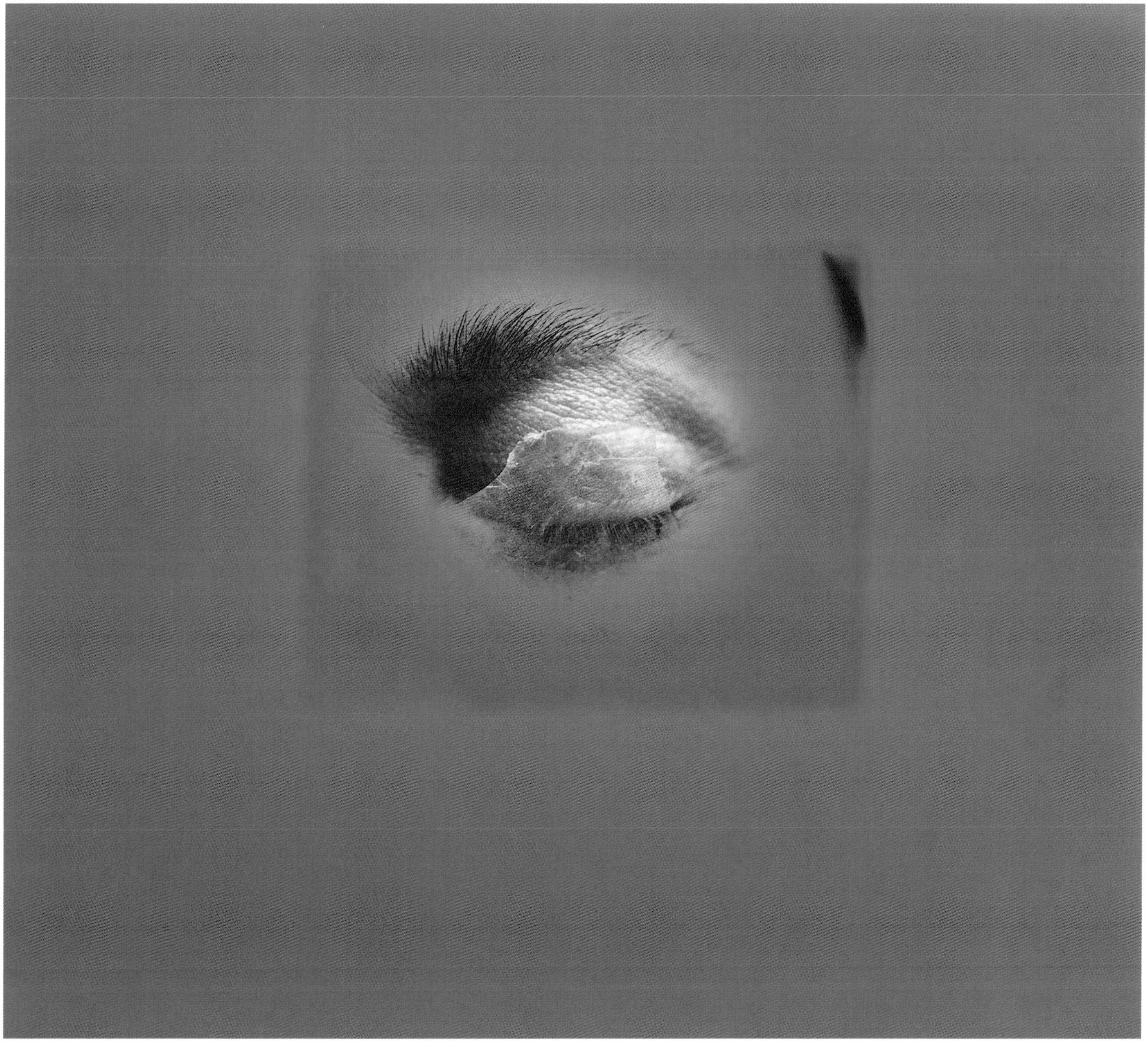

19

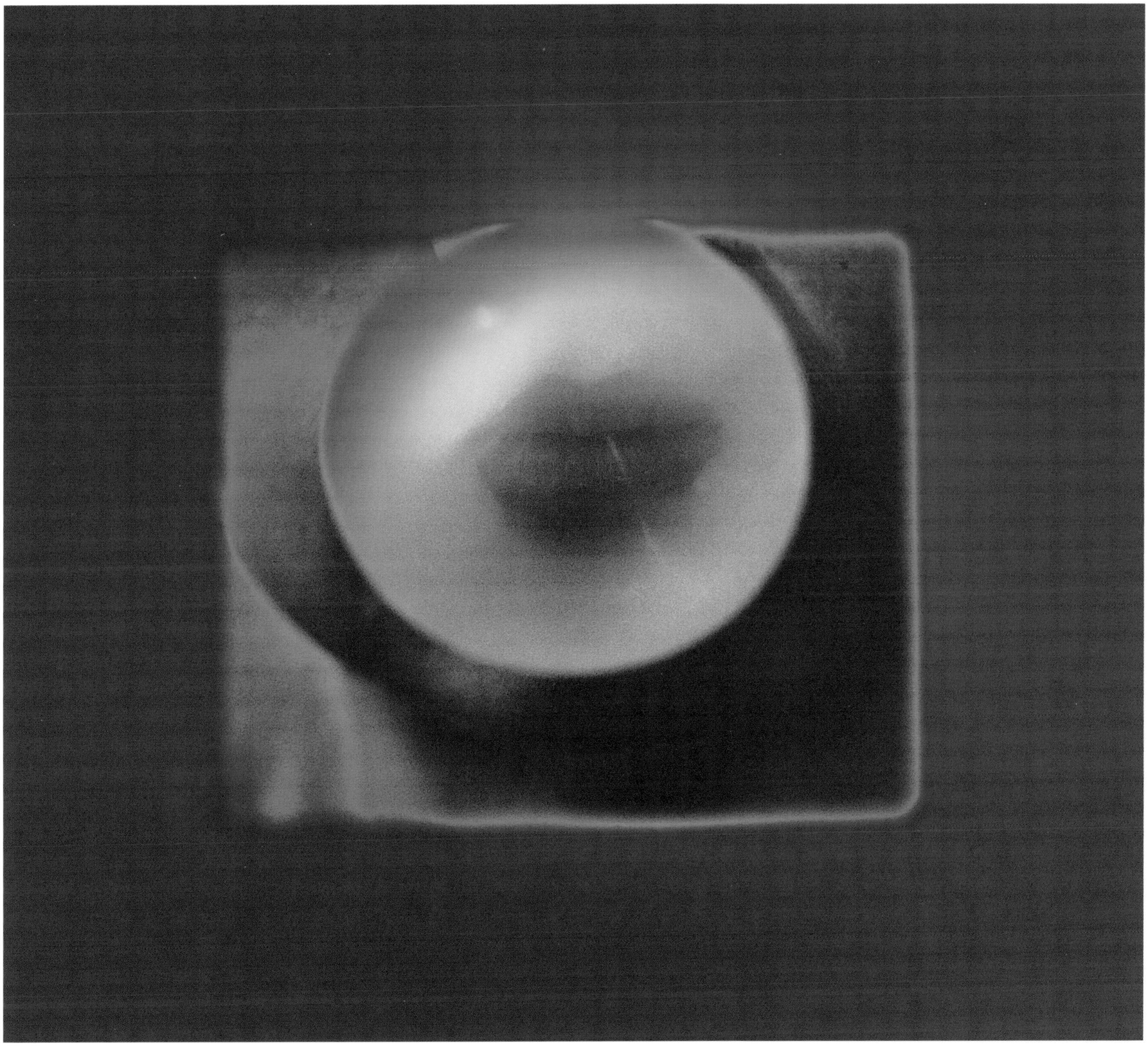

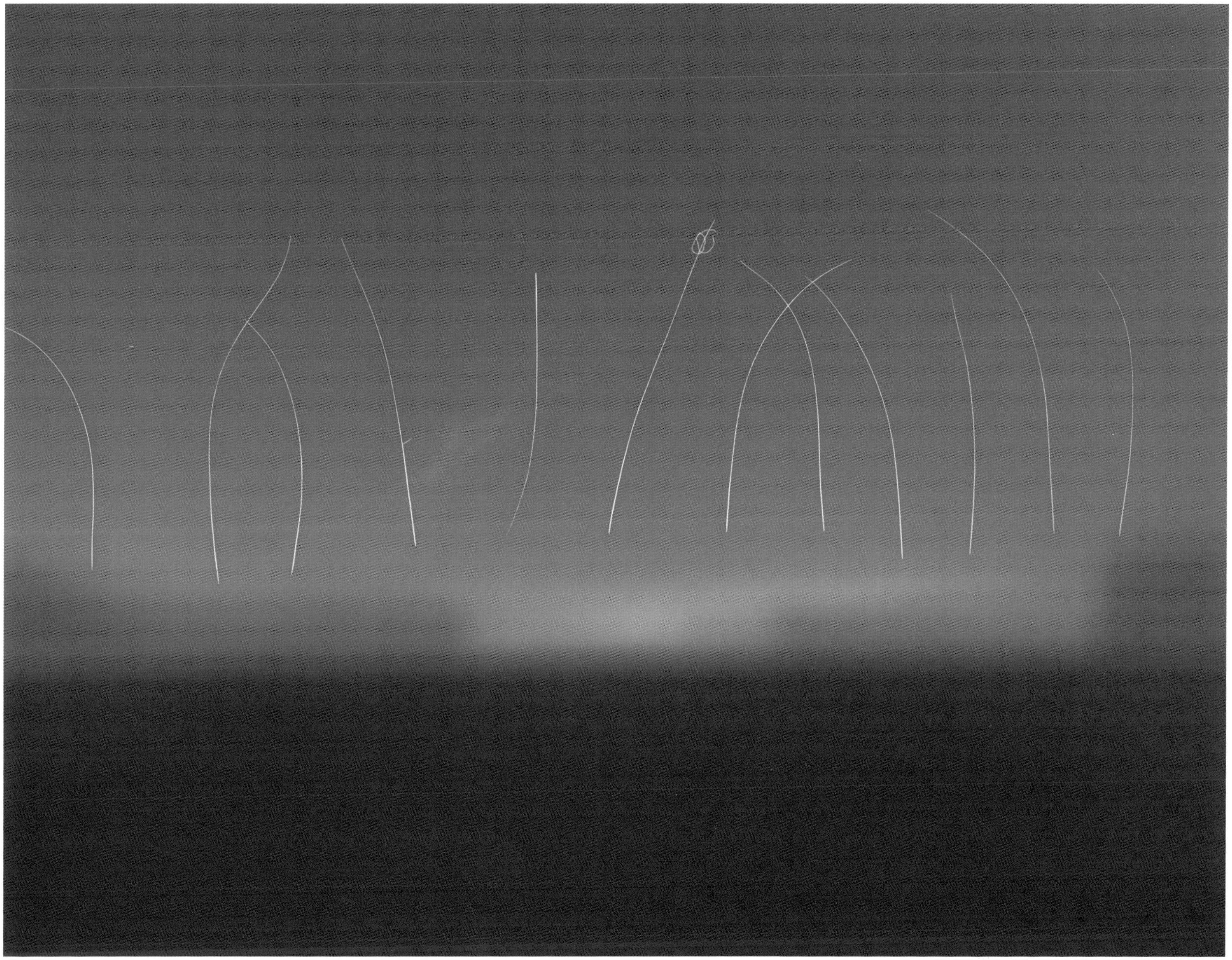

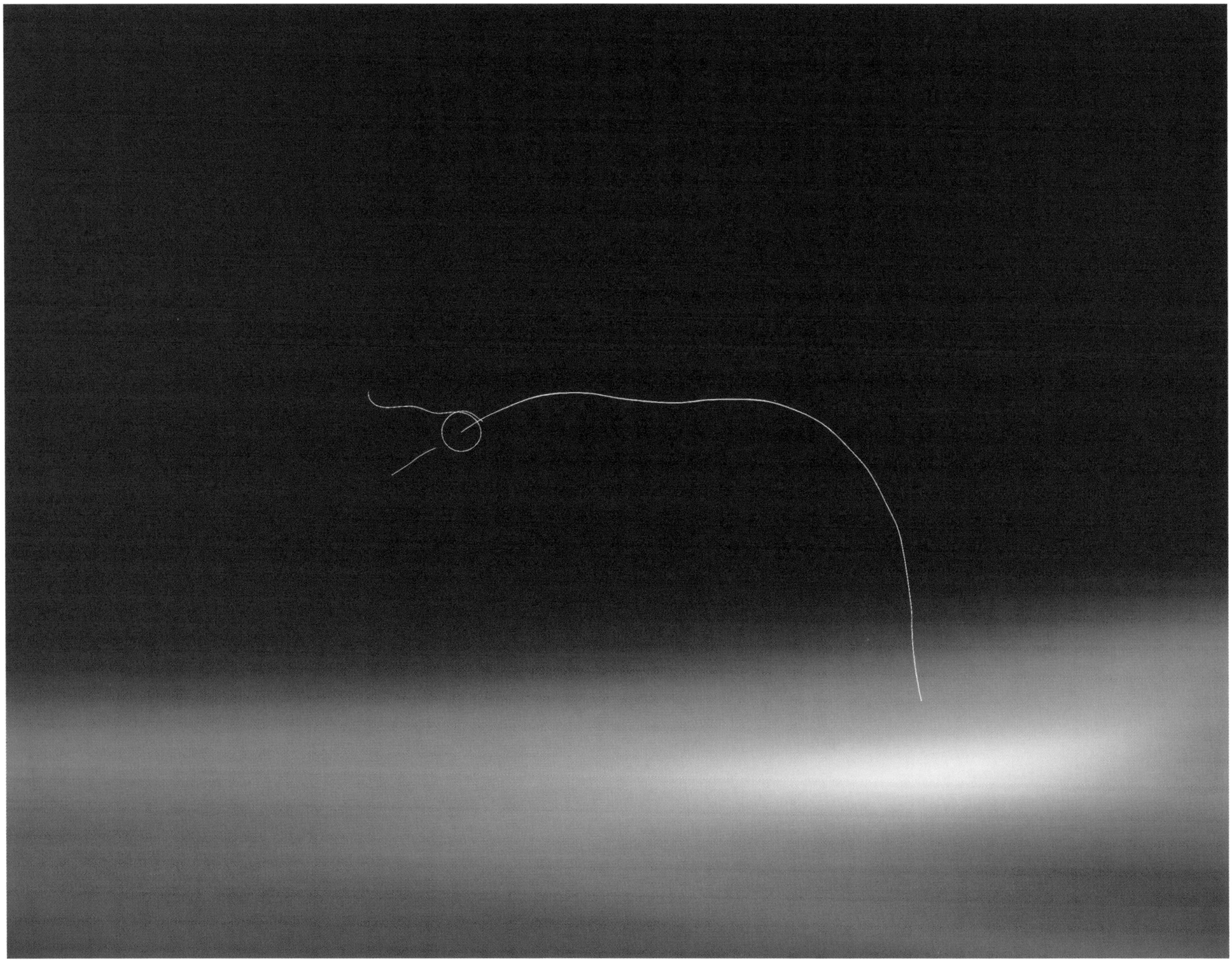

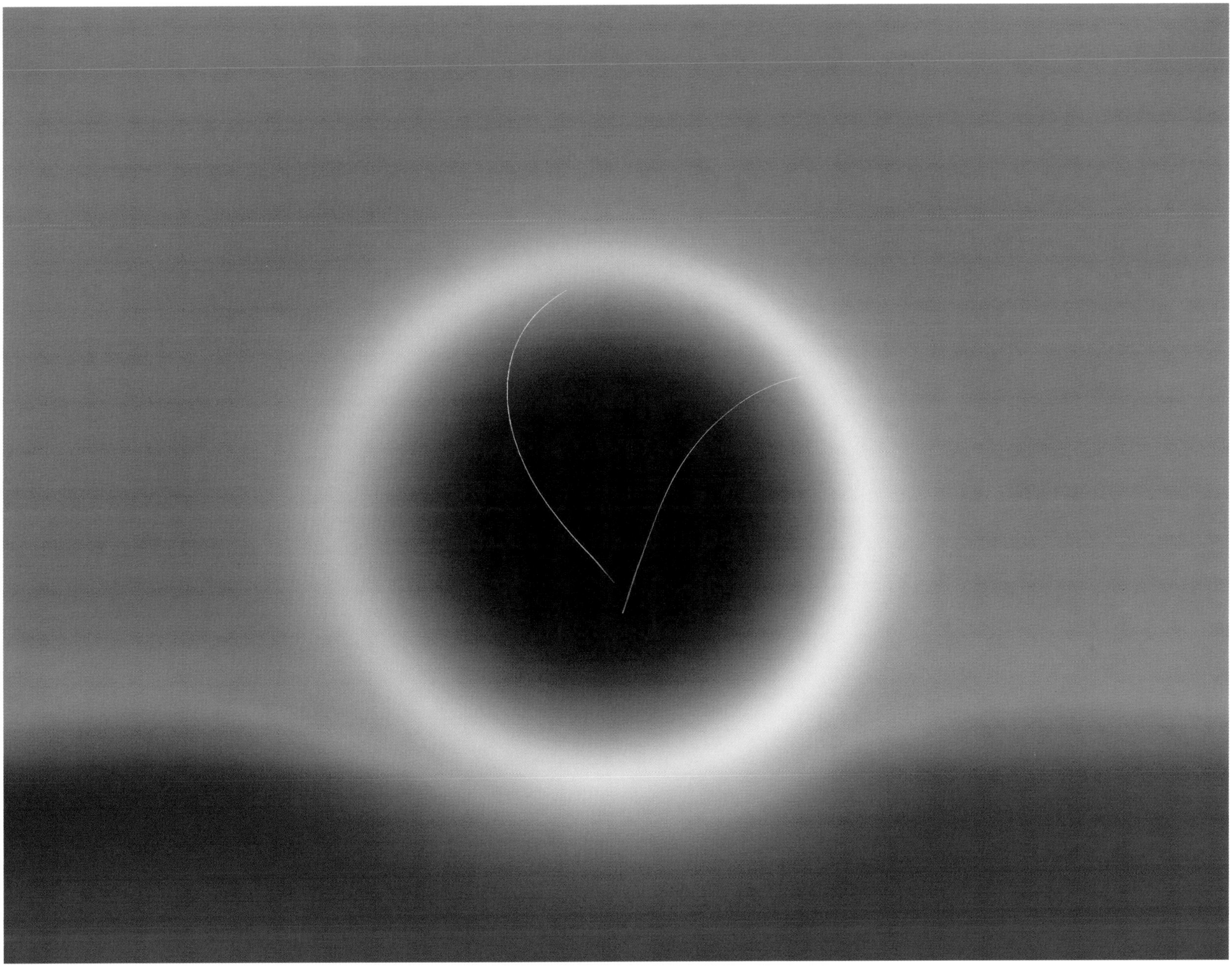

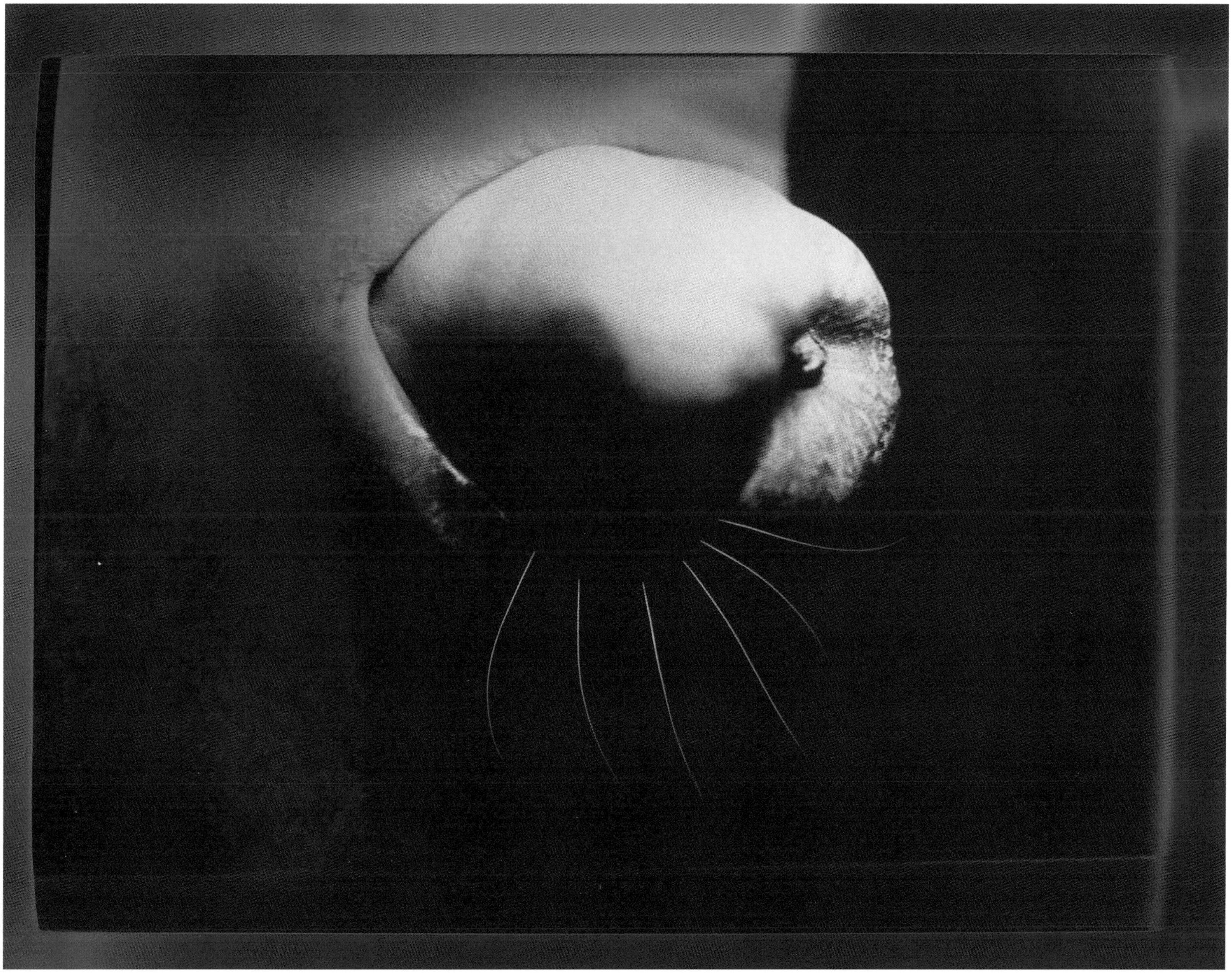

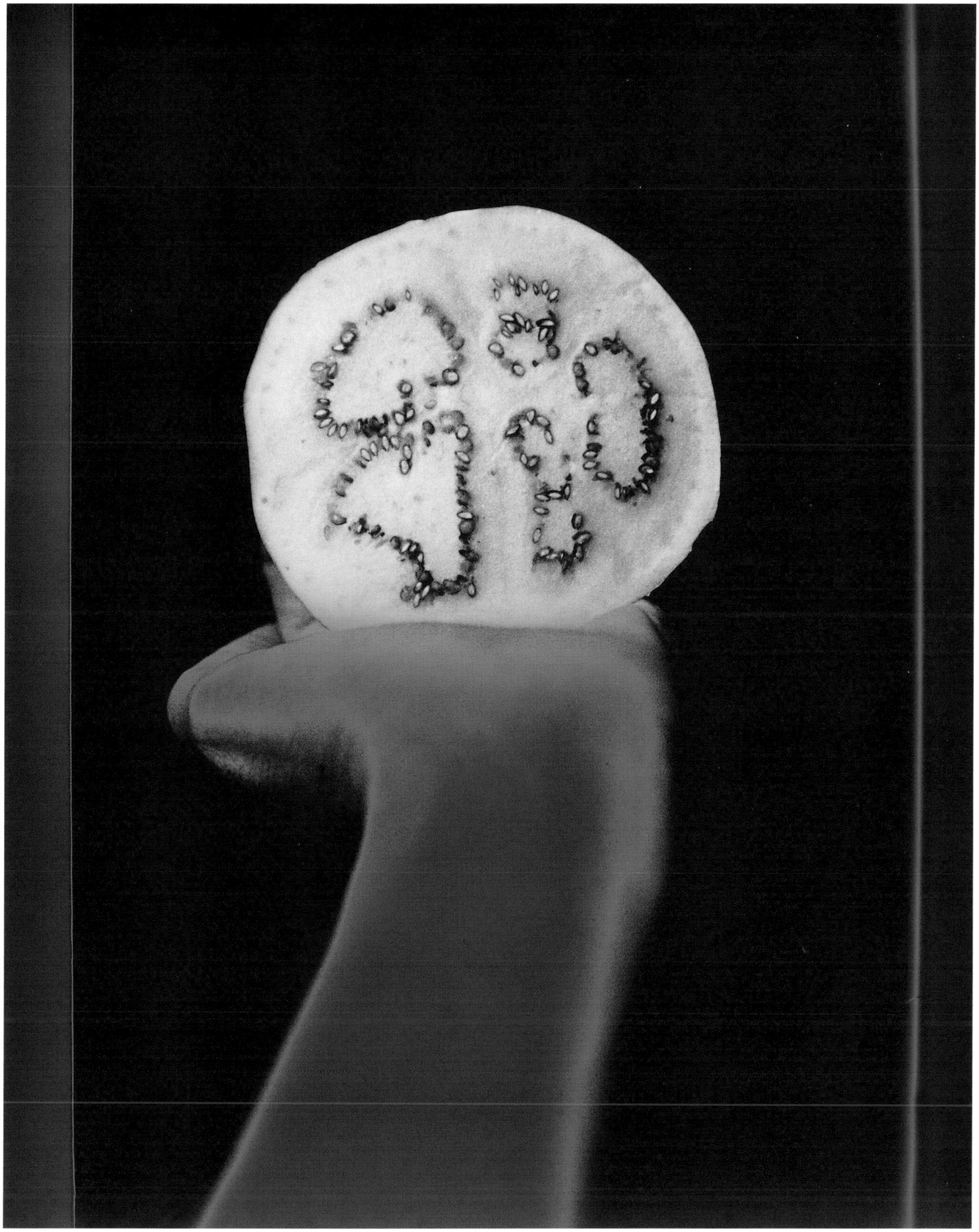

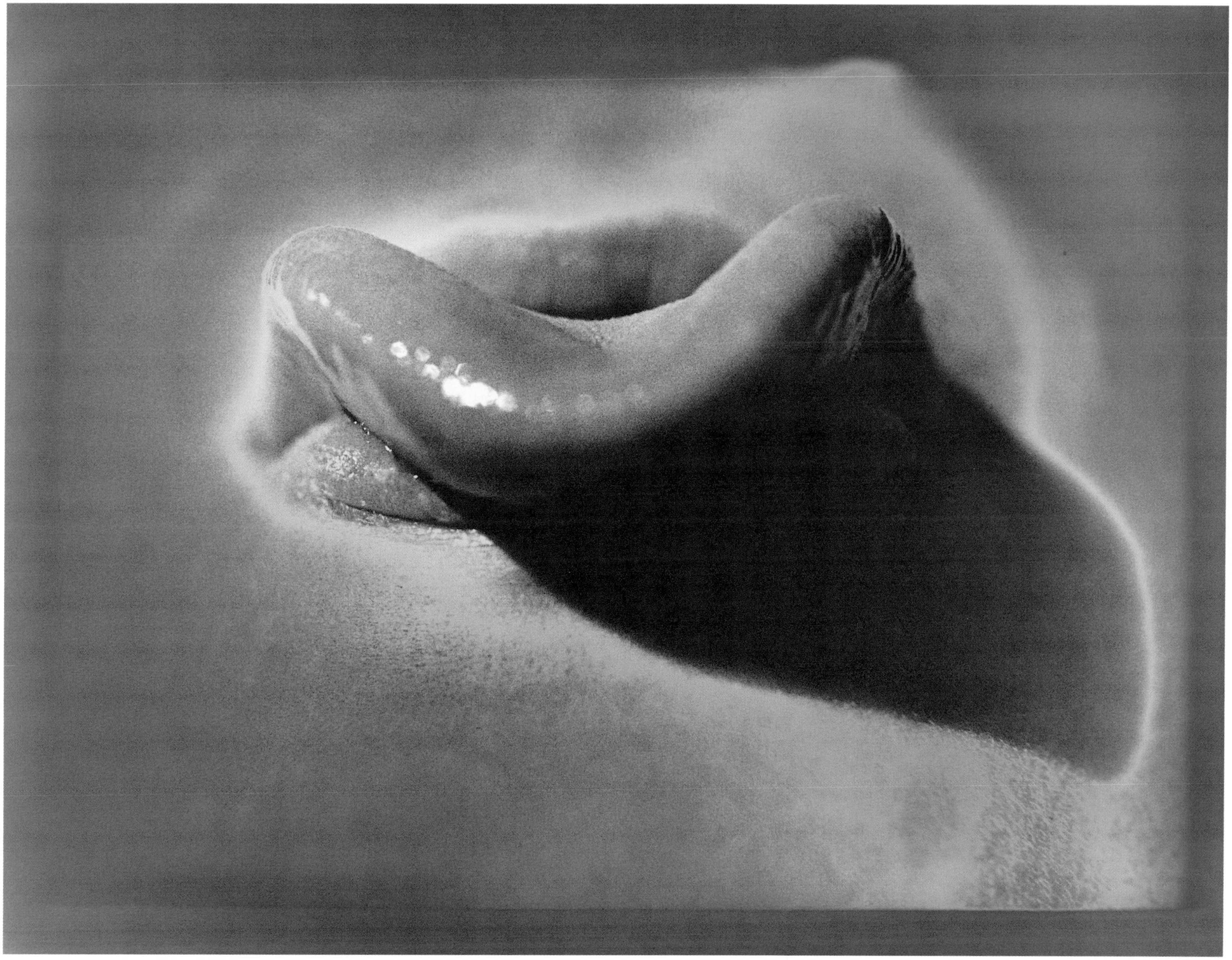

27

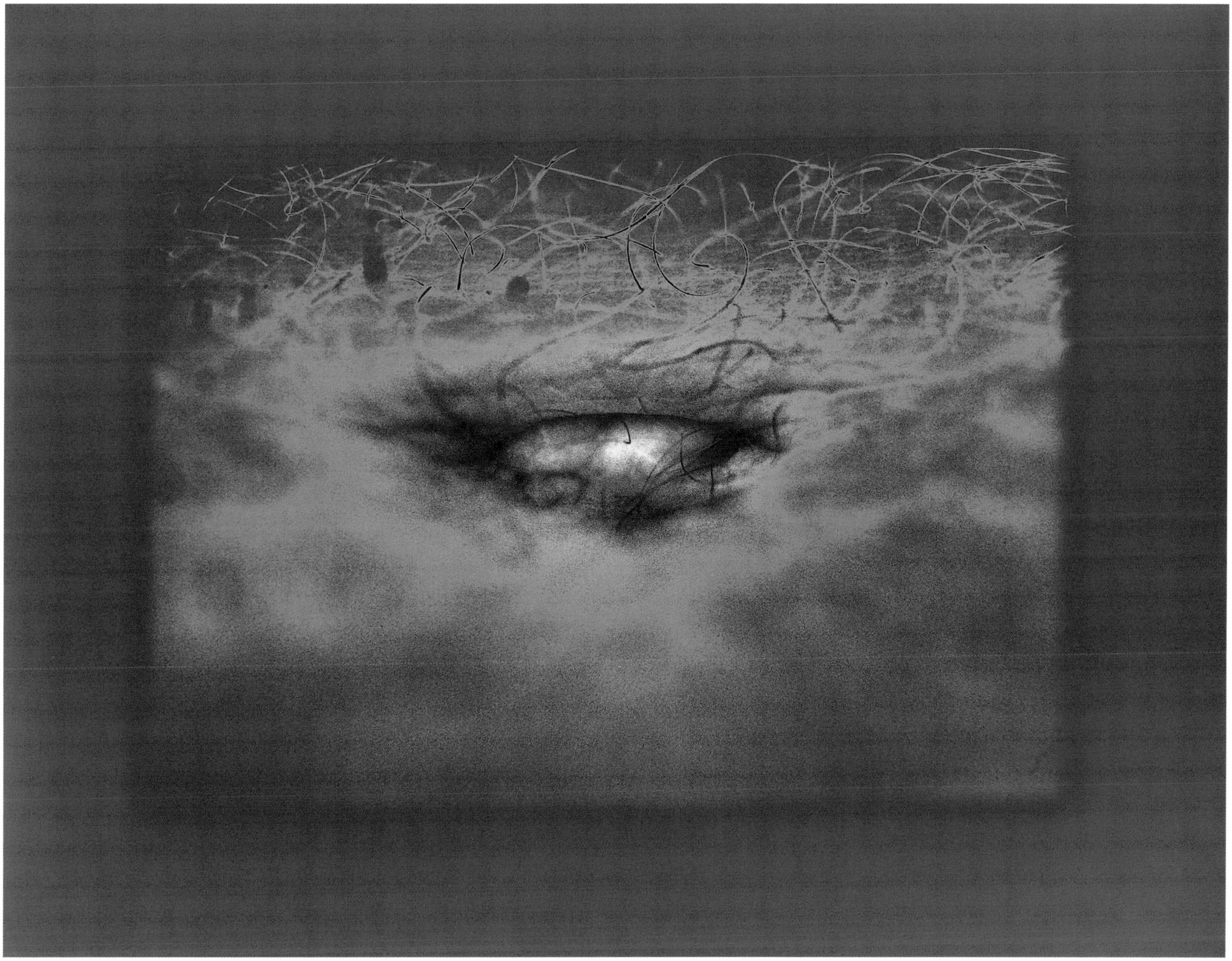

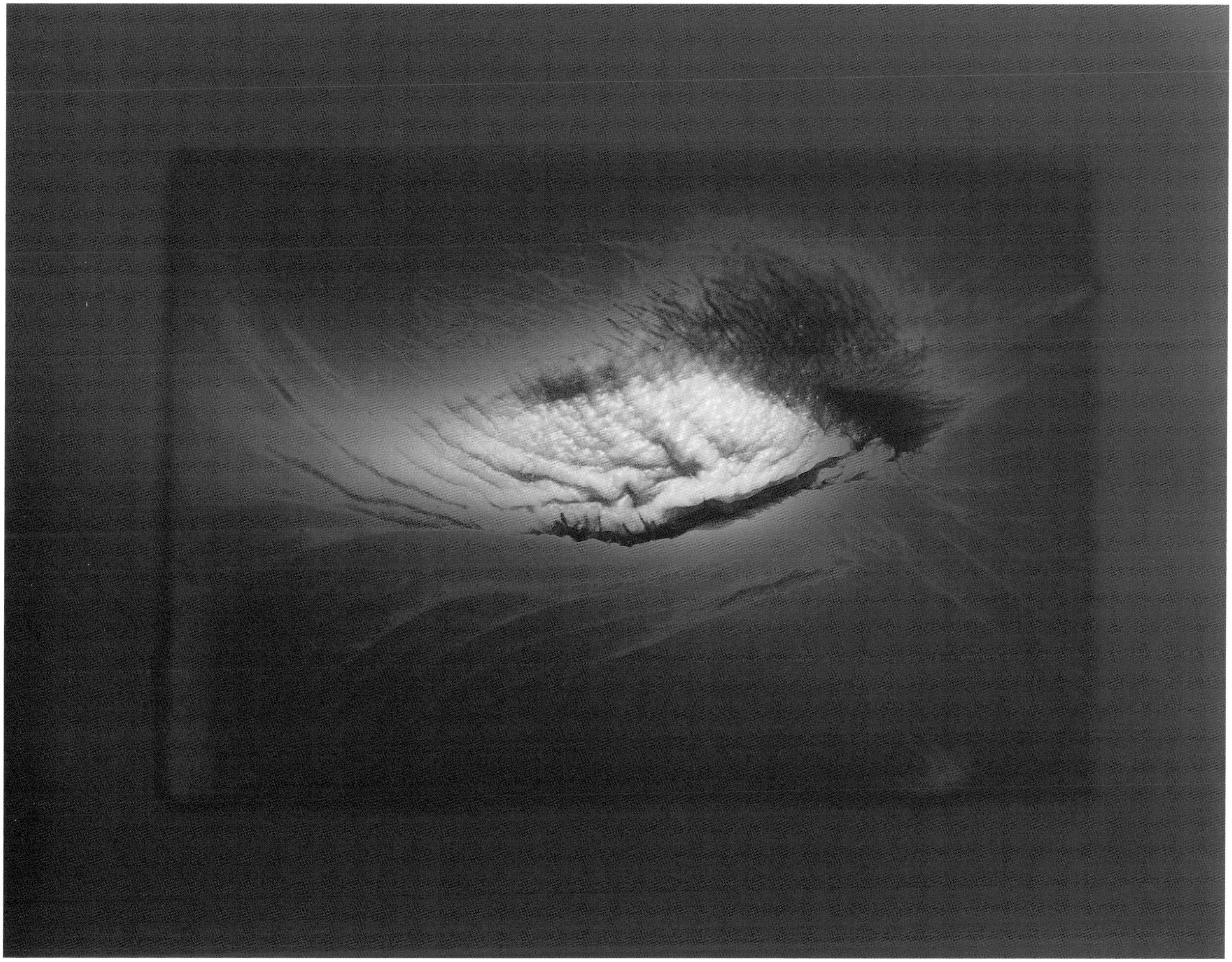

29

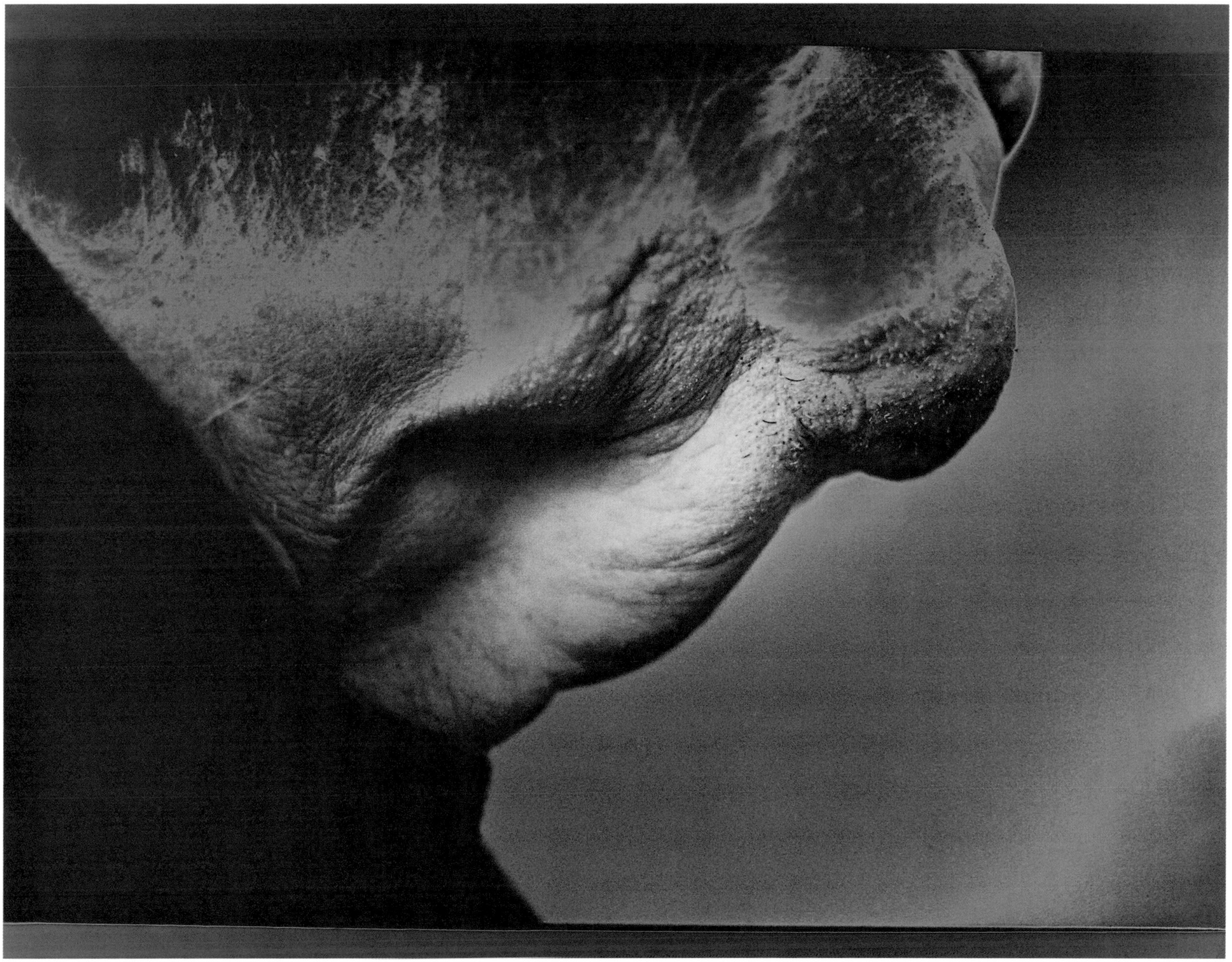

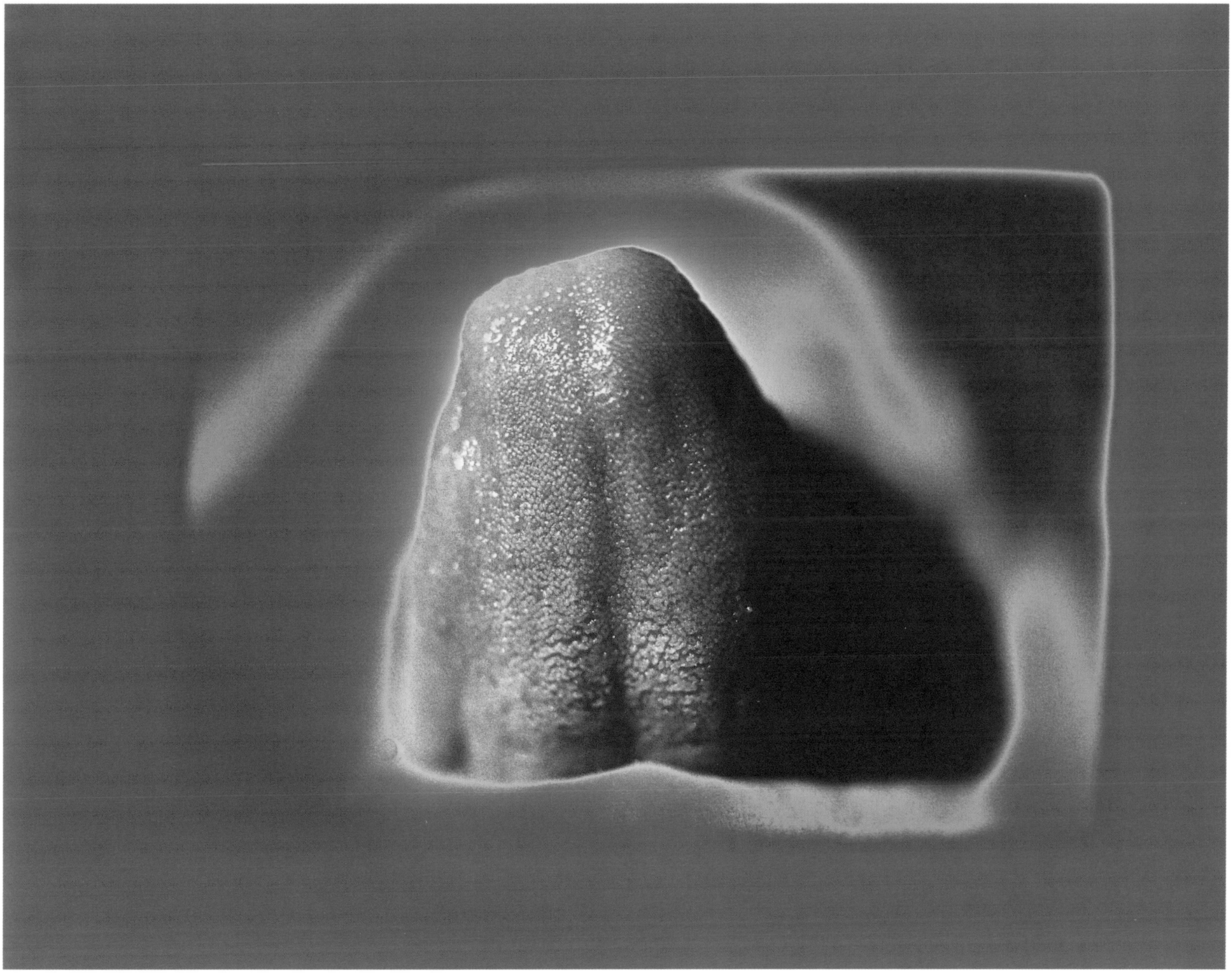

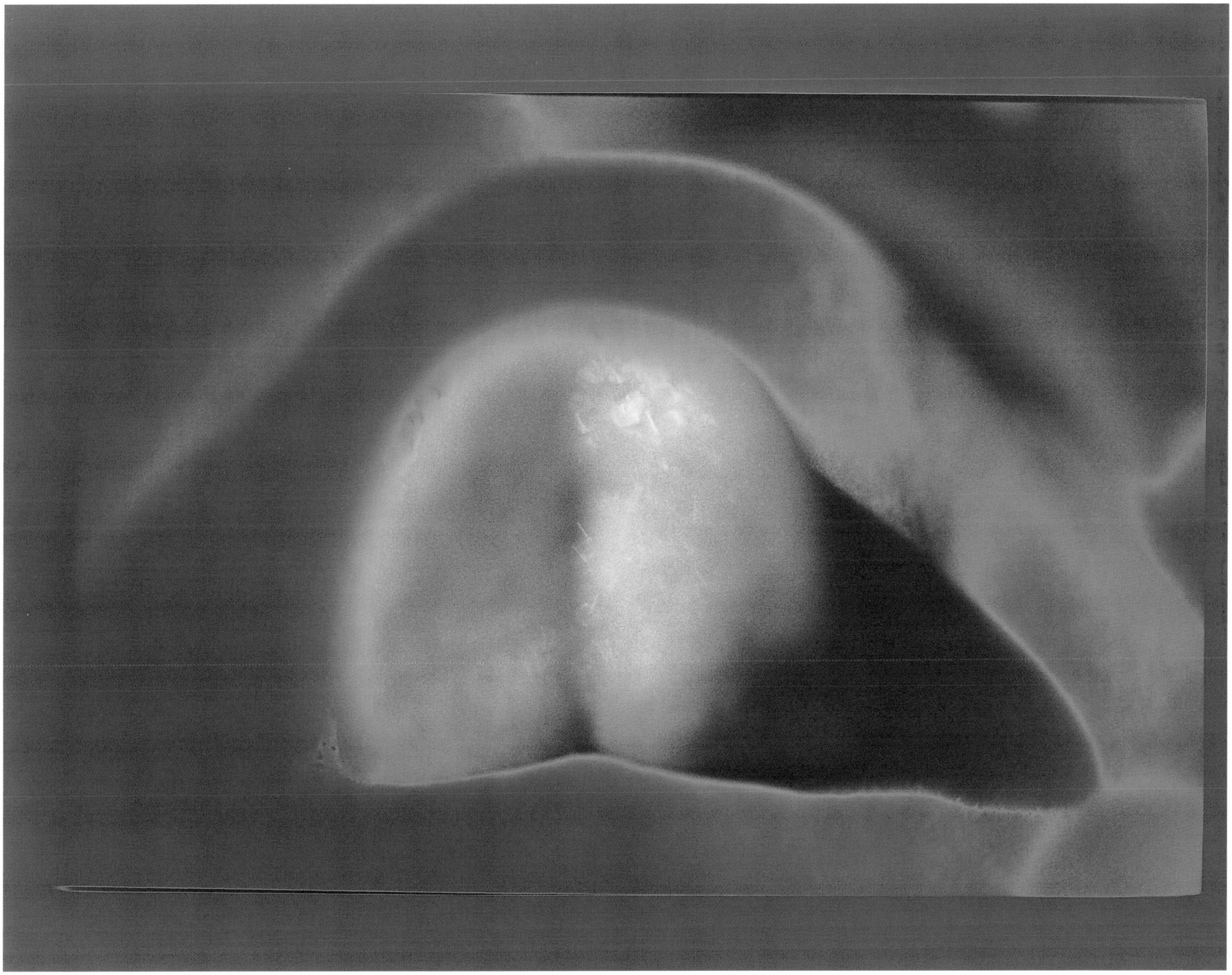

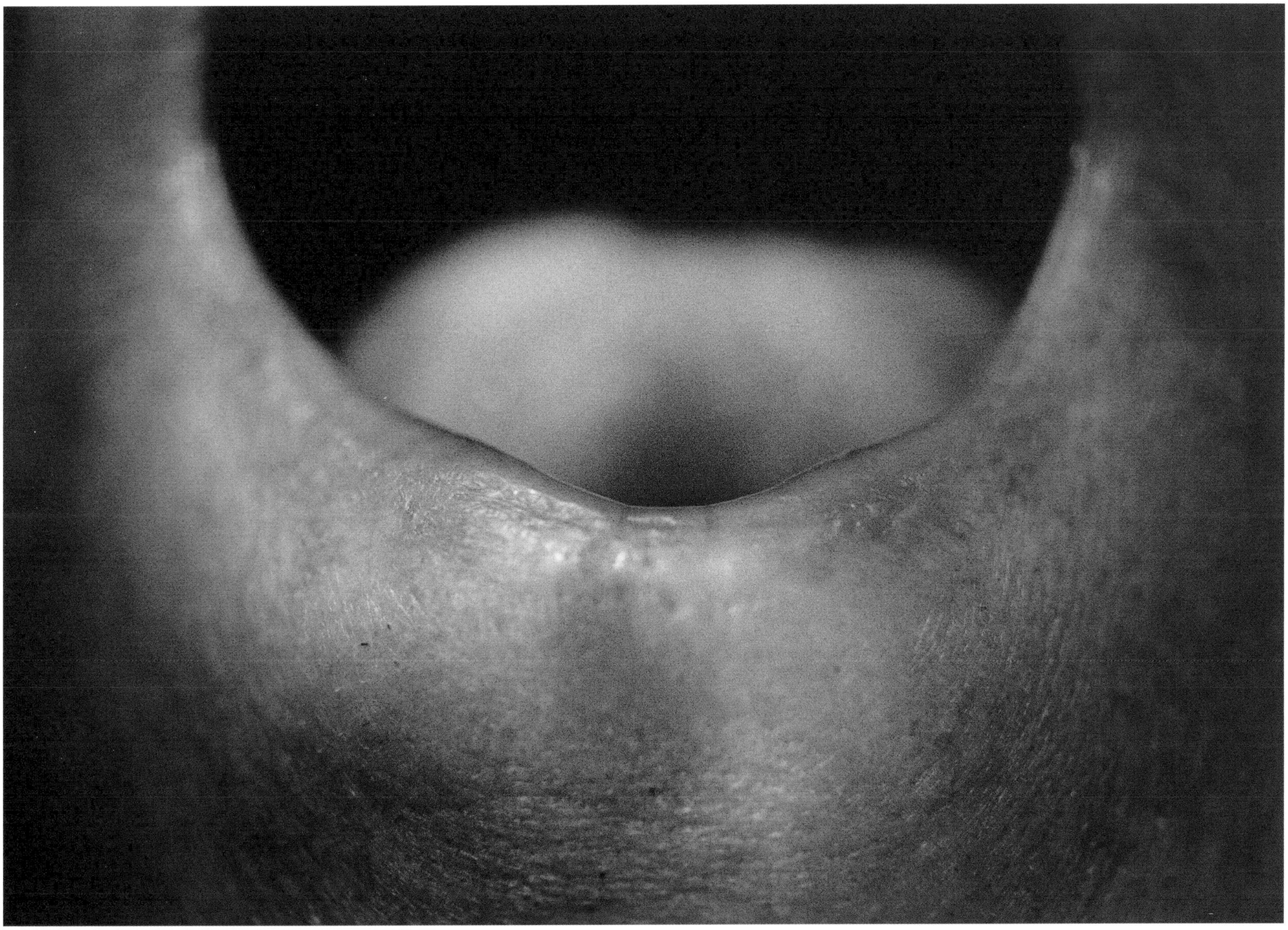

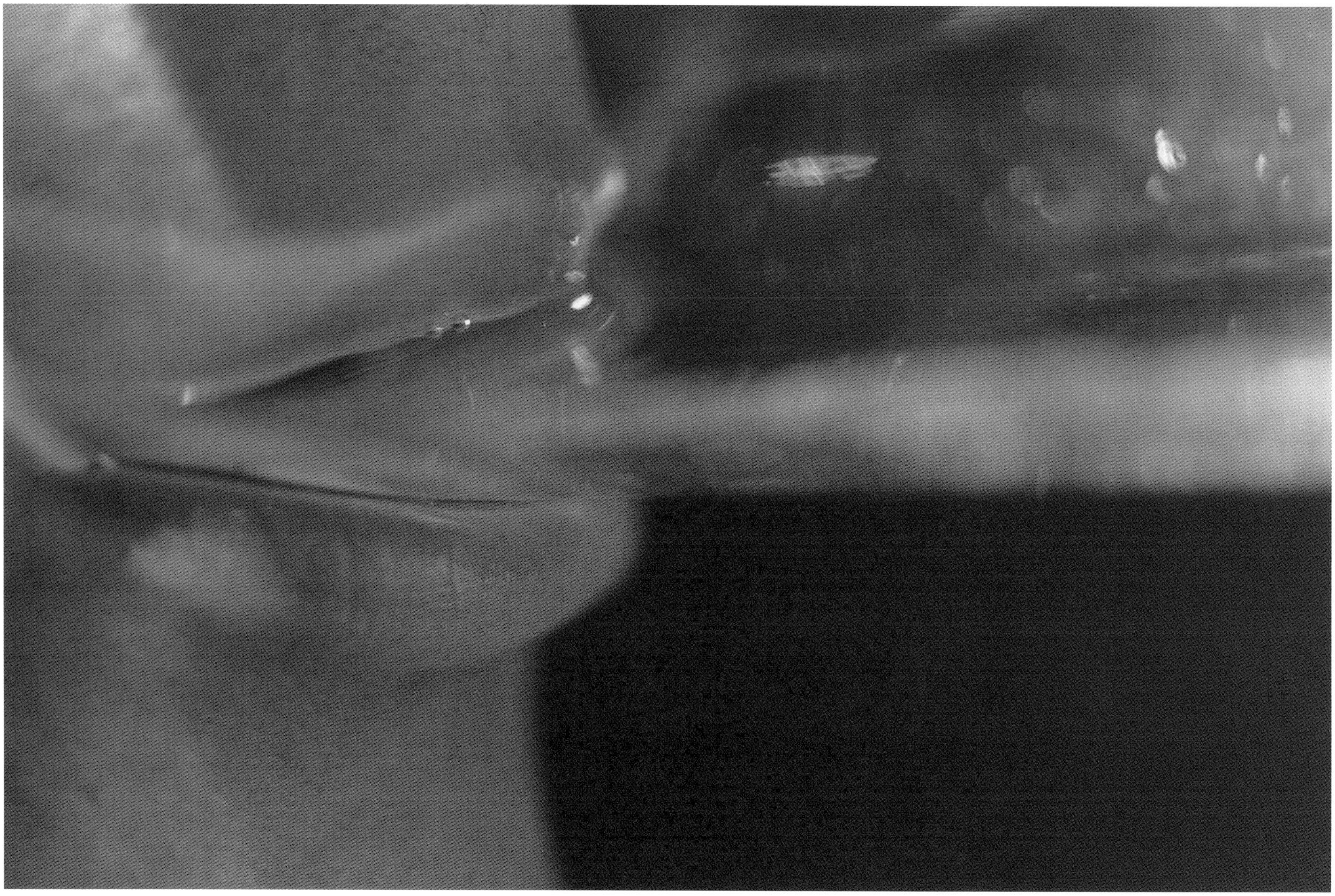

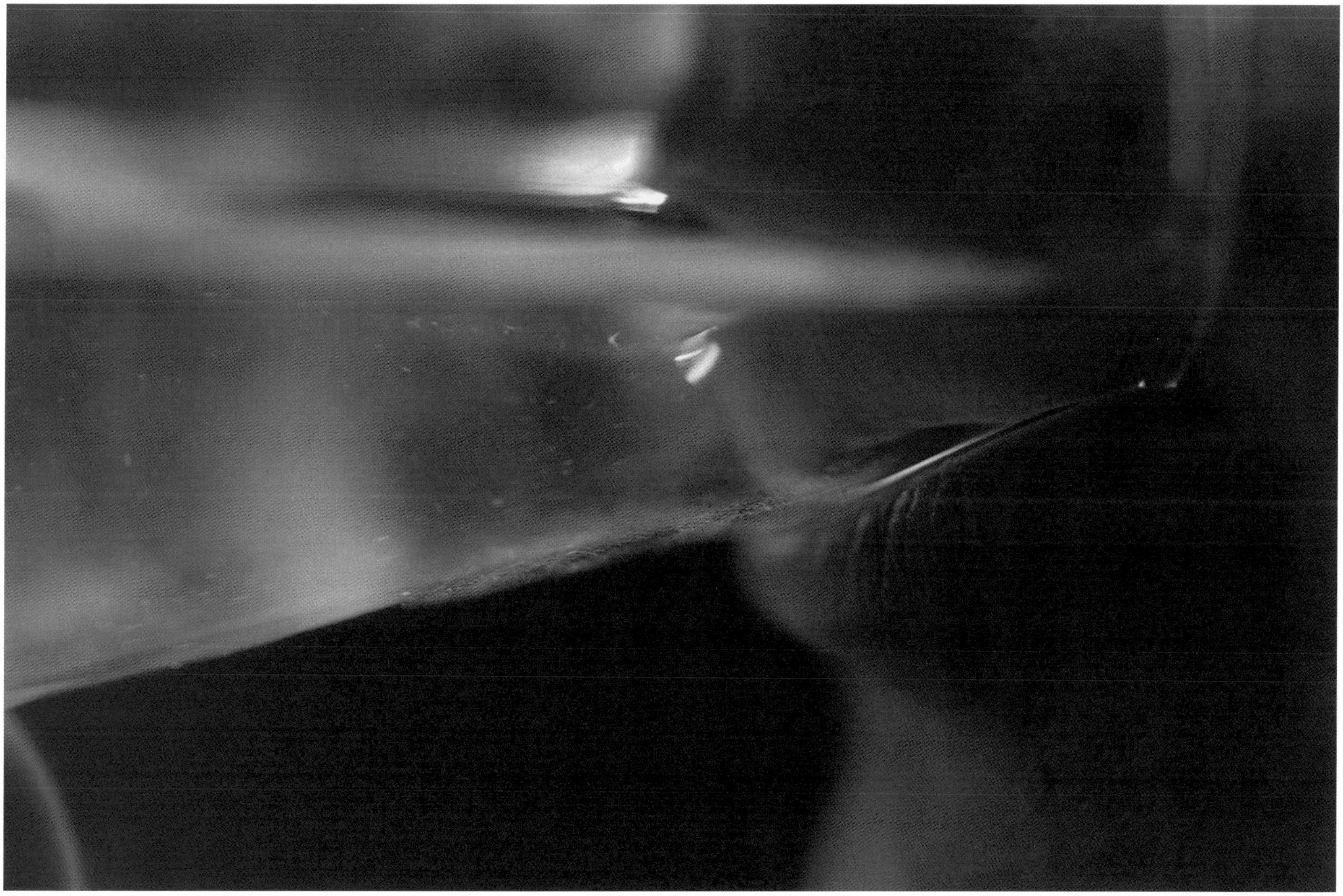

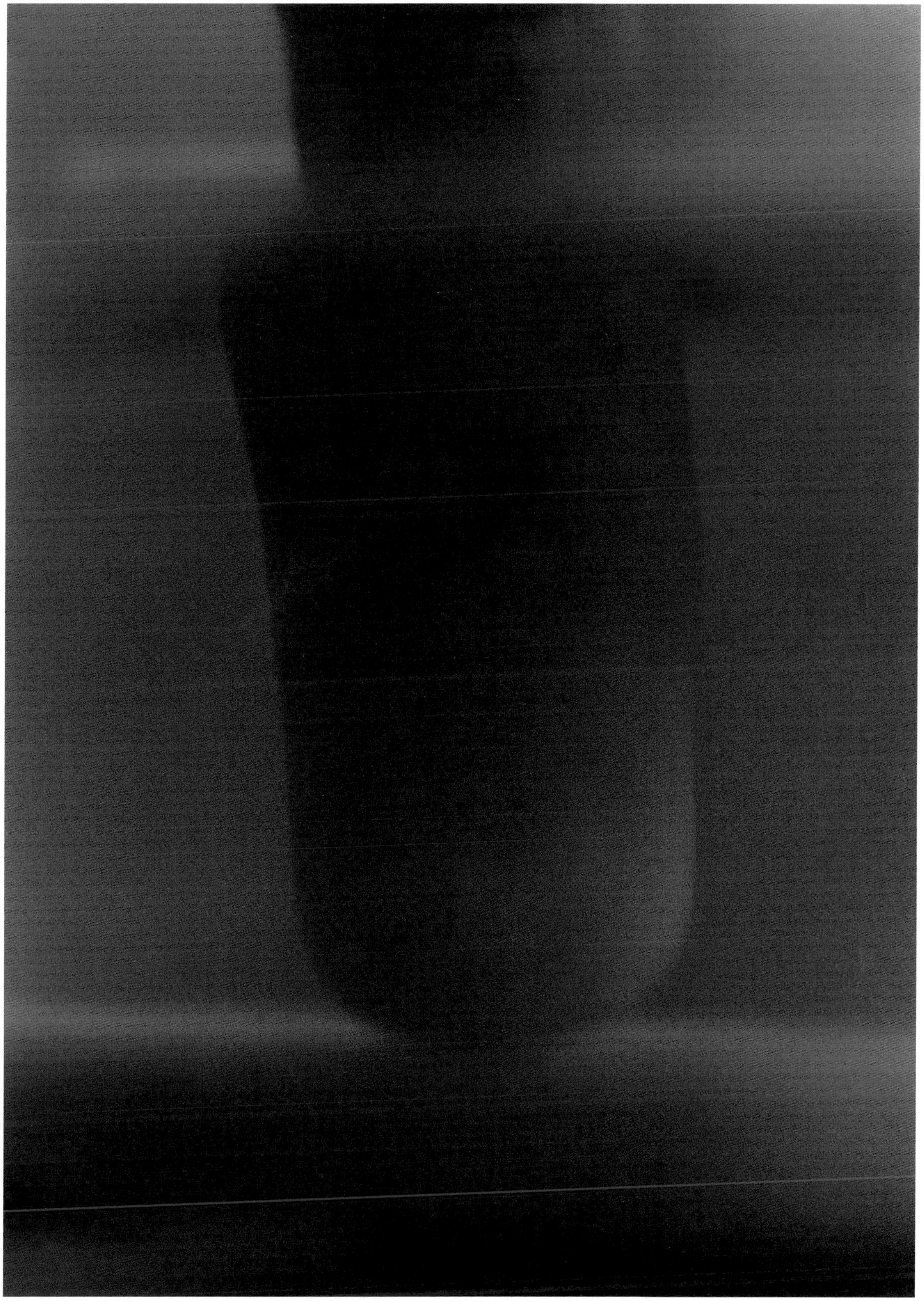

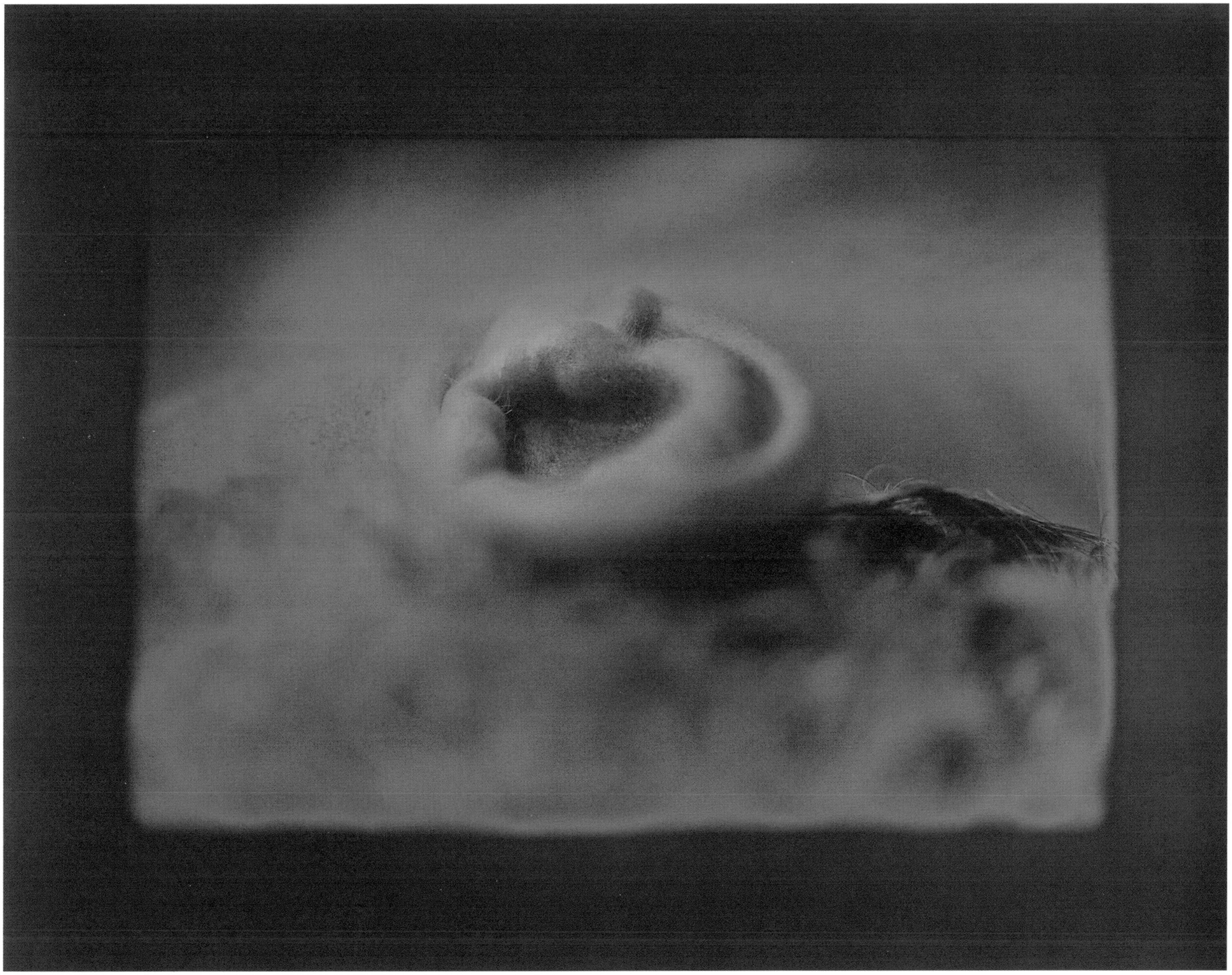

39

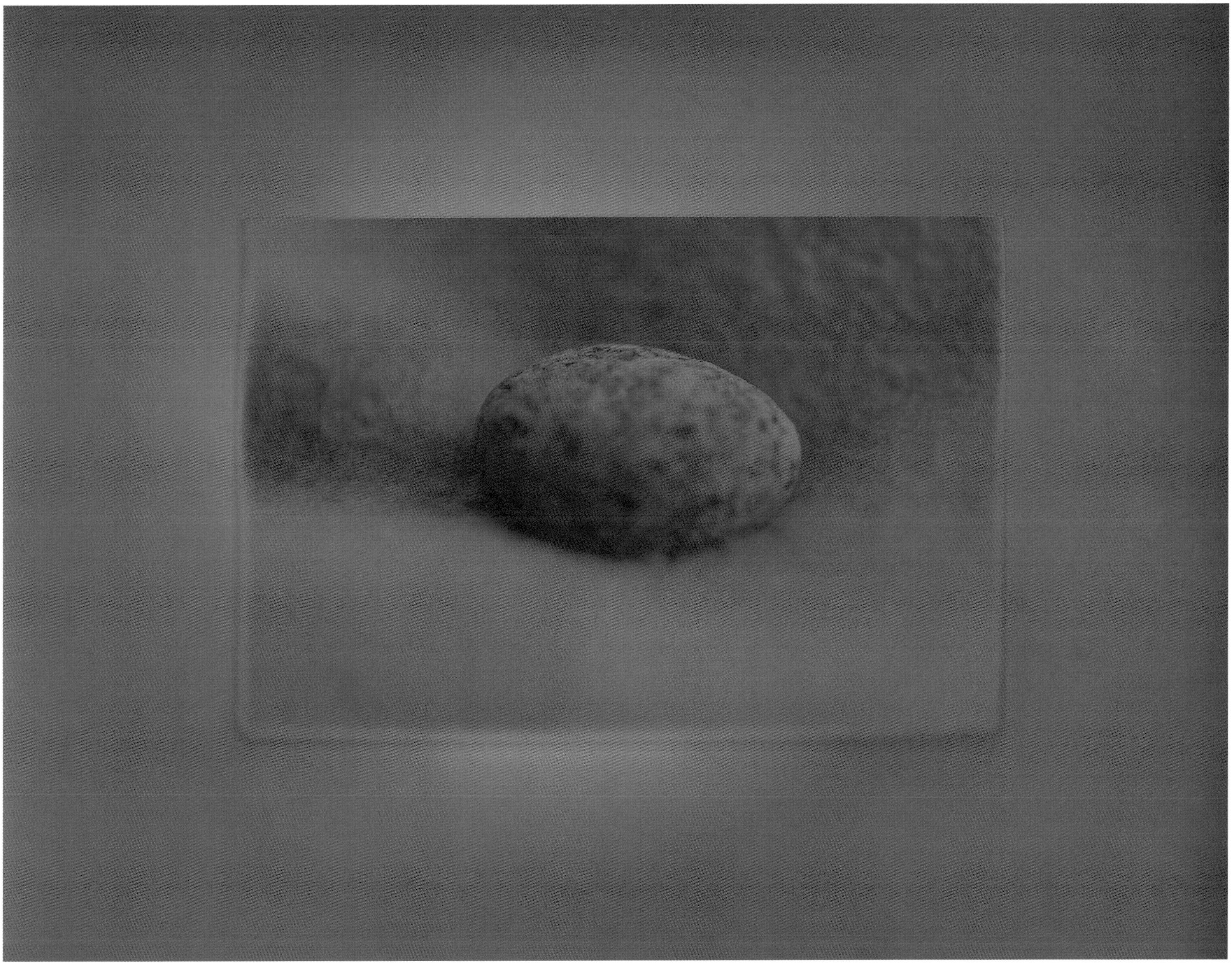

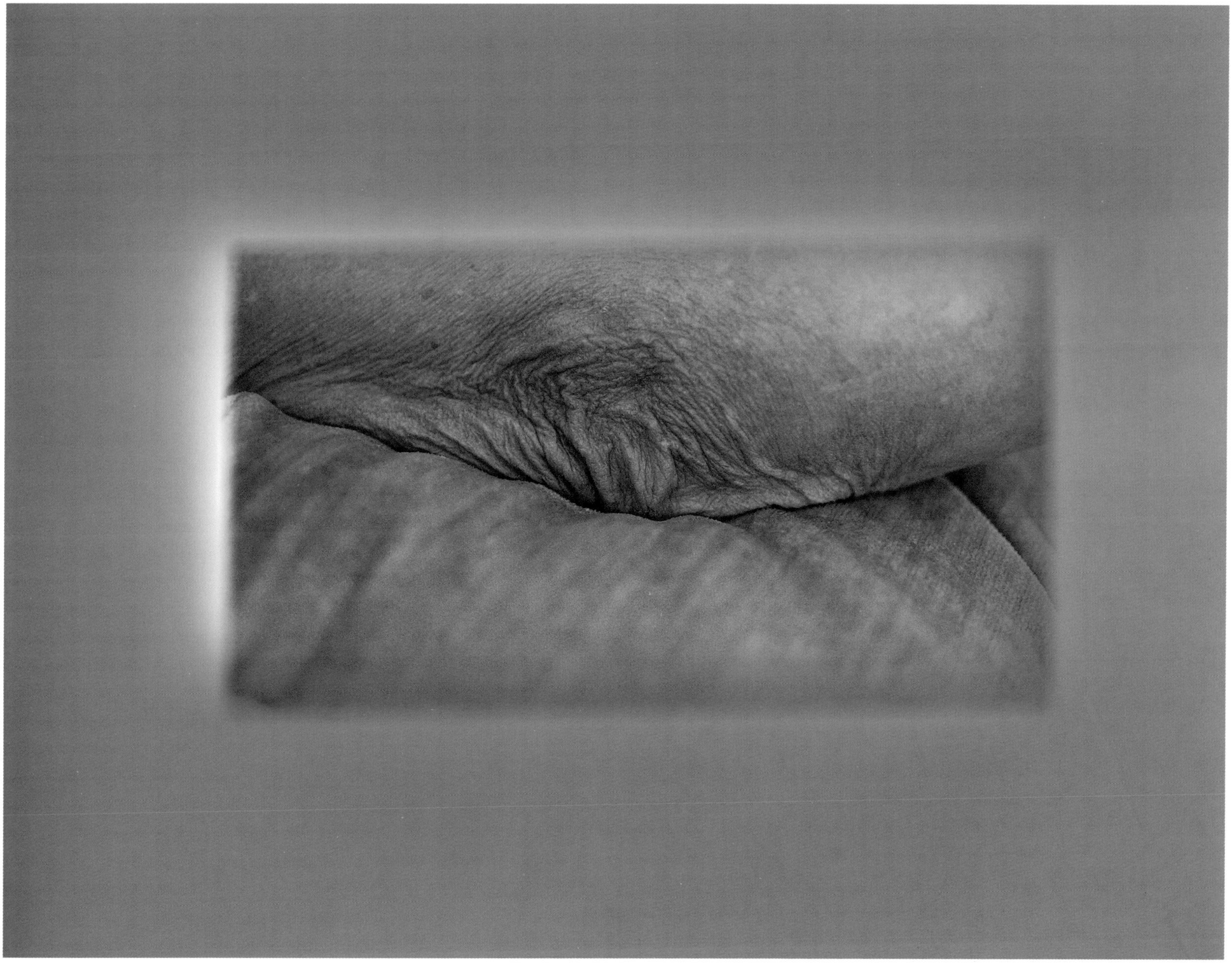

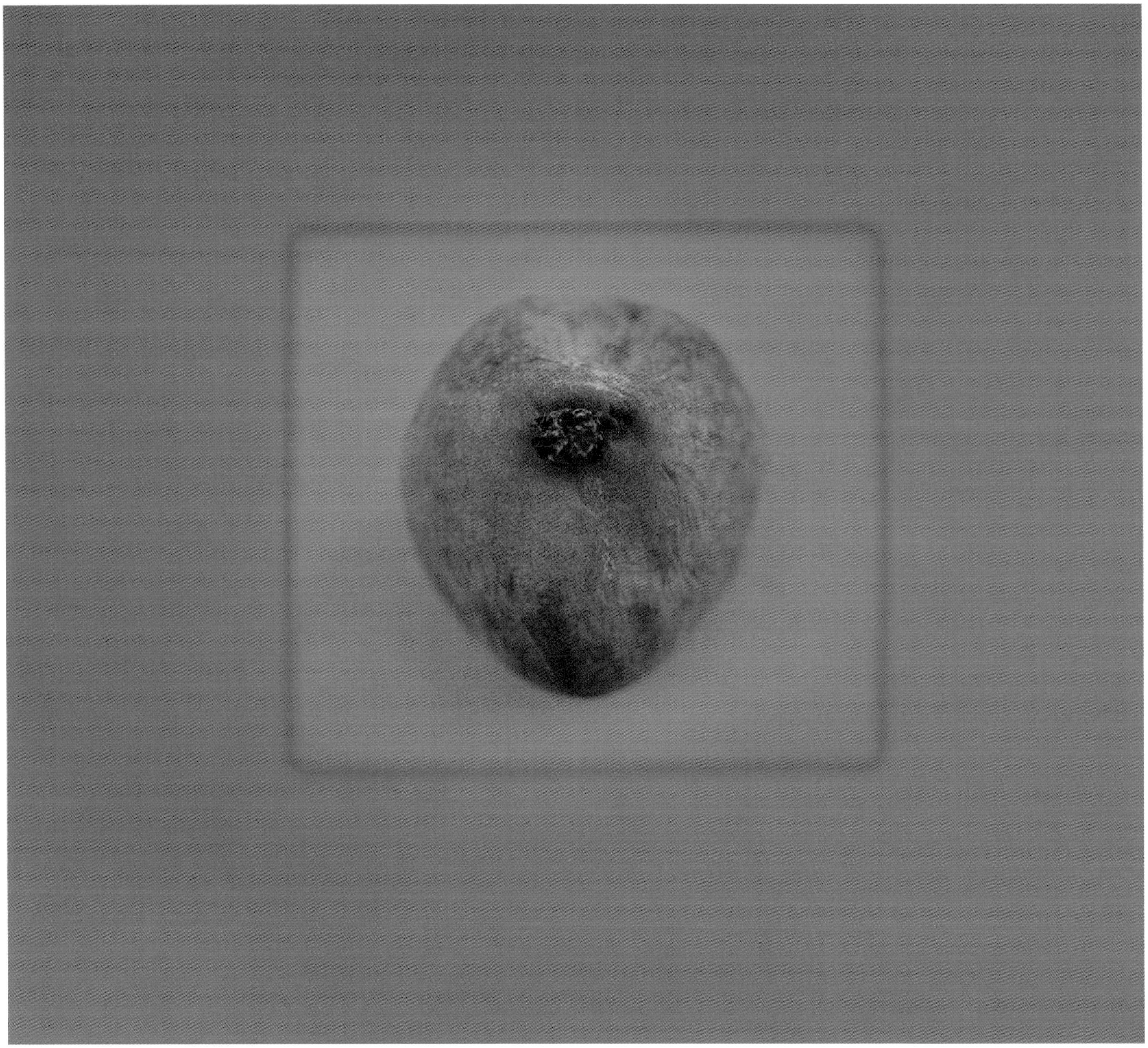

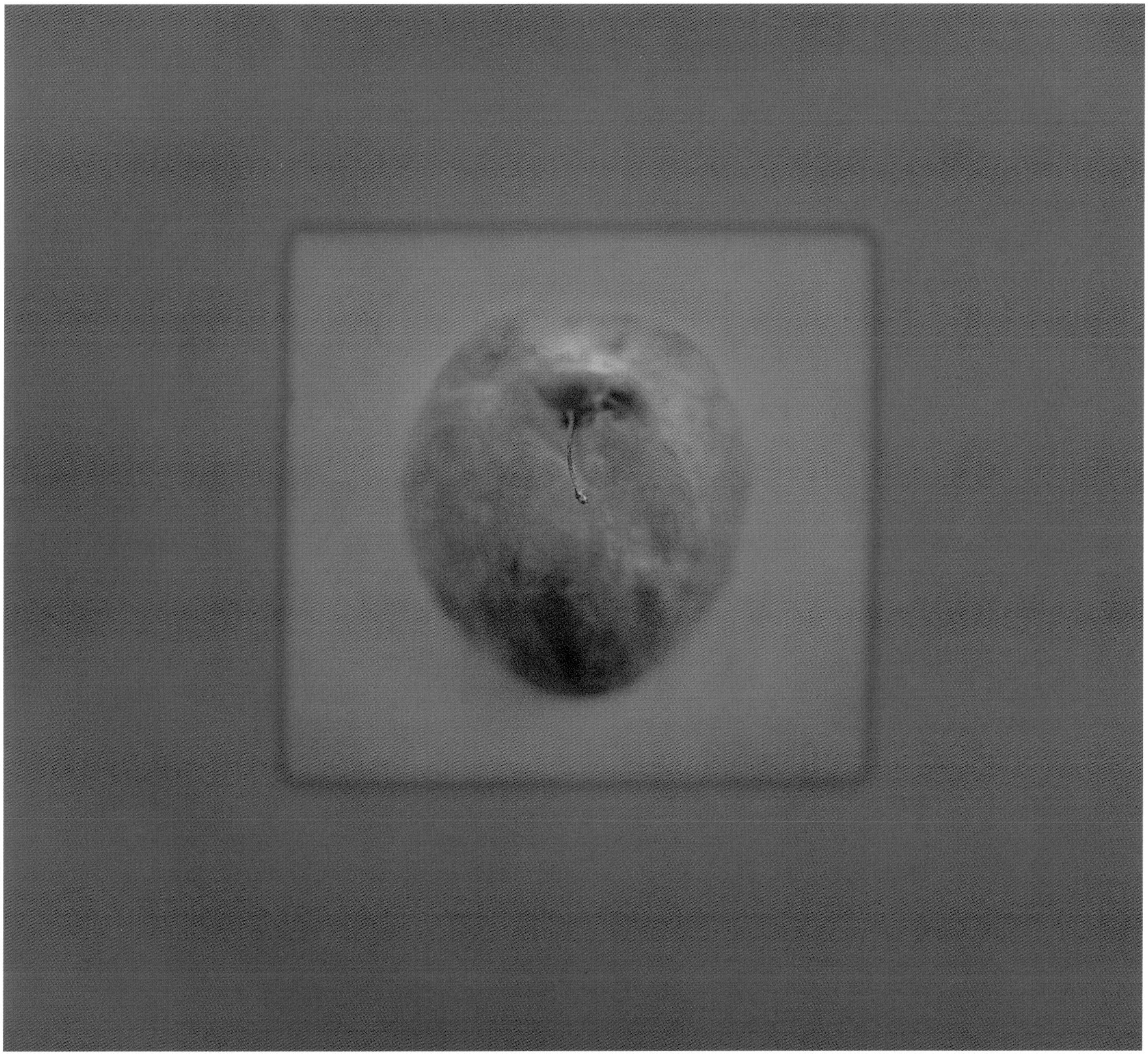

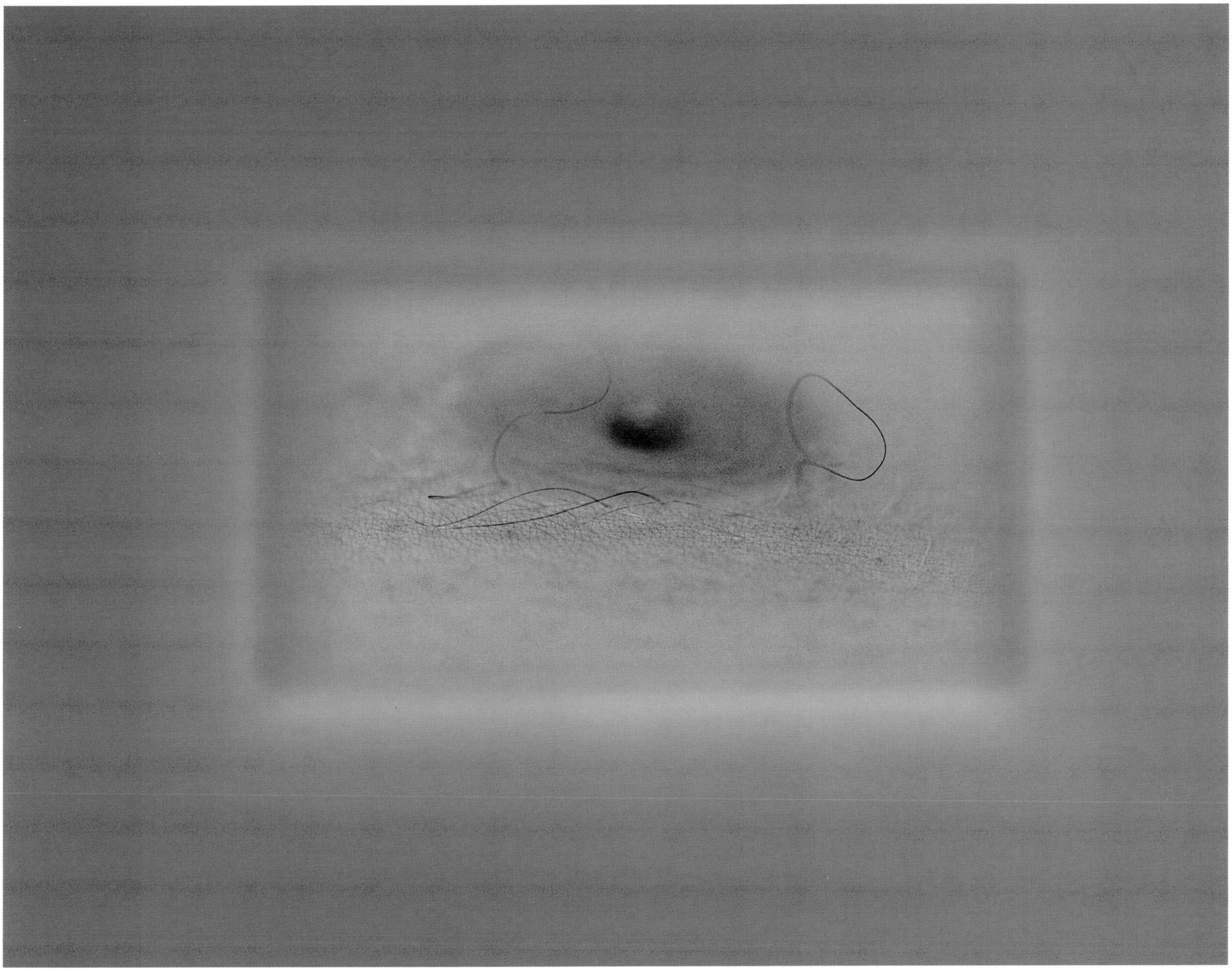

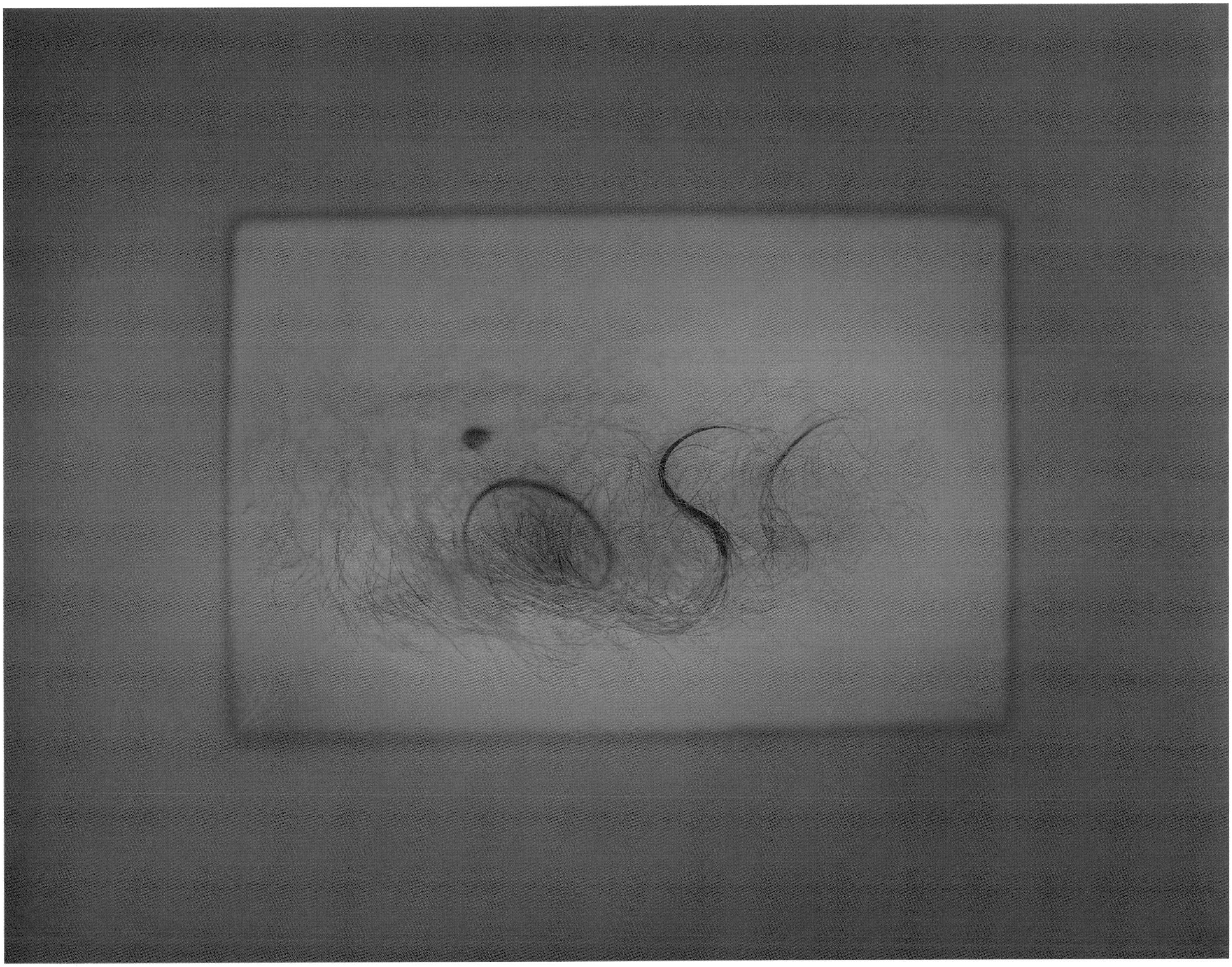

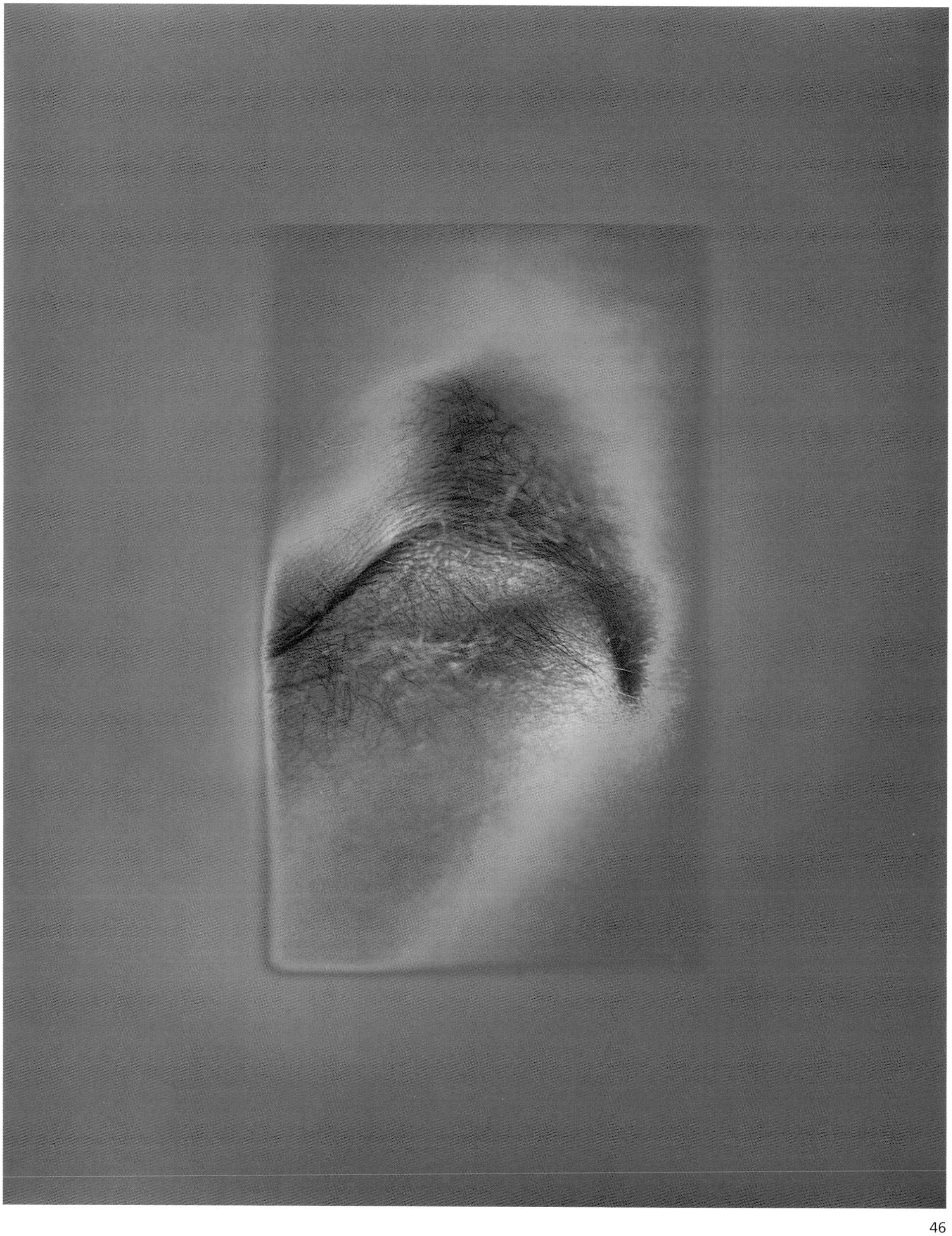

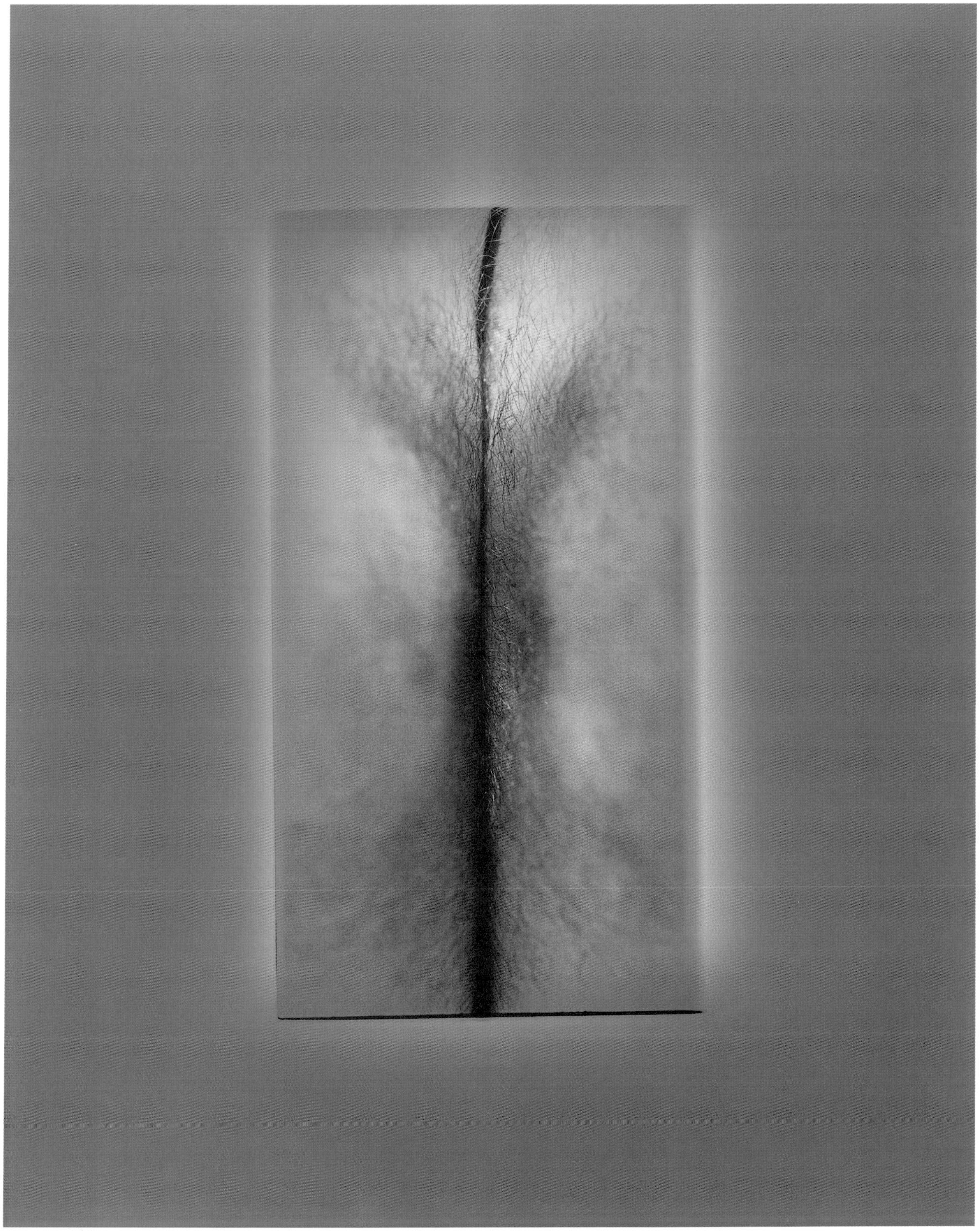

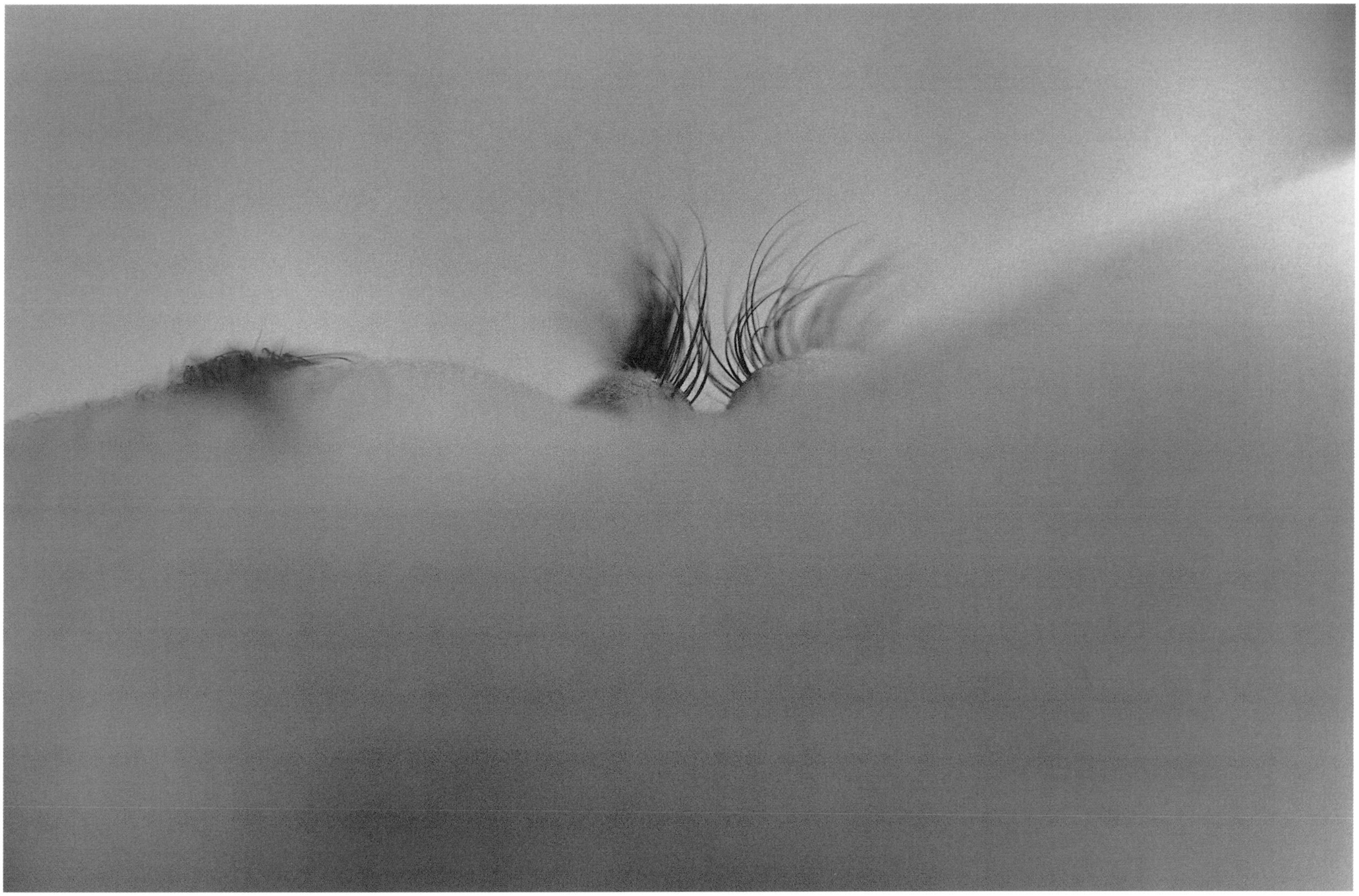

51

Food for Astonishment
Rudolf Schmitz

How should we refer to the photographs of Ann Mandelbaum—as paradoxical emblems? Generally speaking, emblems are understood to be conventionalized images which openly declare their significance and wear their meaning on their shirtsleeves. Below the surface, Ann Mandelbaum's photos do awaken associations with speaking, looking and understanding—at least the obsessive focus on mouths, eyes, tongues and hands is highly suggestive of such things. Yet her treatment of these motifs is anything but conventional. We inevitably notice that mouths are full and eyes closed, that tongues seek escape from mouths and hands or fingers appear to melt with the objects they hold. If these are "speaking" images, their speech is surely impeded or disfigured by some inner stress.

Mandelbaum's photographs are hybrid creatures. They are both mute and communicative at once; they elevate the collage to the status of an organic principle; they experiment with the functional jurisdictions of the senses only for the purpose of propagating the transfer of sensory response; they present abstraction as tenderness and embody an intimate vision of the monumental. Finally, Ann Mandelbaum's works reach back into the history of photography, transforming its alchemist tradition into a perspective on the future.

There's often a paradigmatic link between the origin of the physical body and the space-creating mysteries of the darkroom. Sometimes drops of liquid define a foreground plane, contrasting the suggestion of bottomless palpable space with evidence of an everyday reality devoid of illusion—the laboratory process. What we see here has nothing to do with the myth of a new beginning or creation out of nothing; instead, it is the visual reassessment of existing images involving fragmentation, reassembly and layering: a thoroughly analytical process. It does incorporate some of the gentle touches of fusion, however, of cosmetic corrections made to colliding particles of reality.

The velvety black in which certain motifs are embedded evokes the idea of a kind of probing in complete darkness, accompanied by the appropriate sensations of panic, fright, sudden instinctive retreat and puzzlement in the face of the circumstances and objects one encounters in the process. And then there are the walls of fog, created with the aid of soft-focus or solarization, in which some clearly delineated motifs dissolve into abstraction. The areas of sharp focus appear stuck in these veils of cloudy objectivity like thorns in flesh, like shrill tones that are swallowed and absorbed as they spread towards the edges. At the point at which gray fog begins to stretch clearly defined objects over the planar surface and into nothingness, the factual findings become overwhelming. A mouth grows uncontrollably towards a wall, an eye expands into a lake and a bulging fruit becomes a towering mountain. In moments such as these, Ann Mandelbaum's photographs assume the authority of dream: The object-organs are overpowering, the monstrosities inescapable, the appeals impossible to ignore.

In photographs such as that of an open mouth containing a bitten-off piece of a chocolate caramel, the idea of a simulated slur of the tongue is both amusing and irritating at the same time. One has an impression of the tongue as a bodiless sense organ poised at the threshold between swallowing and articulating a word and refusing to budge. Mouths, lips, eyes, tongues and ears are parts of the body concerned with boundaries, with points of

Ann Mandelbaum

Born 1945 in Wilkes-Barre, Pennsylvania.
Lives in New York.
Currently Adjunct Associate Professor of Photography, Pratt Institute, Brooklyn, New York.

Education

1963–1967
Connecticut College, New London, Connecticut.
B.A. in Spanish.

1976–1978
New School for Social Research, New York.
M.A. in Media Studies.

1986–1990
Pratt Institute, Brooklyn, New York.
M.F.A. in Painting.

Selected Solo Exhibitions

1998
Jackson Fine Art, Atlanta, Georgia

Center for Creative Photography, Tucson, Arizona
Fotomuseum, Münchner Stadtmuseum, Munich, Germany
Stadtgalerie Saarbrücken, Saarbrücken, Germany
Musée de l'Elysée, Lausanne, Switzerland
AR/GE Kunst, Bozen/Bolzano, Italy
Southeast Center for Contemporary Art, Winston-Salem, North Carolina
(travelling exhibition—through the year 2000—and monograph)

1997
Galerie Françoise Paviot, Paris, France
Ubu Gallery, New York

1996
Rena Bransten Gallery, San Francisco, California
Paul Kopeikin Gallery, Los Angeles, California

1995
Aberdeen Art Gallery, Fotofeis, Aberdeen, Scotland
Grey Art Gallery, New York

1994
Frankfurter Kunstverein, Frankfurt/Main, Germany
Espace Photographique Contretype, Brussels, Belgium
Westfälischer Kunstverein, Münster, Germany
(travelling exhibition and monograph)

1993
Le Parvis, Tarbes, France
Bibliothèque Nationale, Paris, France
Galerie J.P. Lambert, Paris, France